9.22.81

WORKING WITH HISTORY

WORKING WITH HISTORY

The Historical Records Survey in

Louisiana and the Nation, 1936–1942

Burl Noggle

Louisiana State University Press
Baton Rouge and London

Designer: Patricia Douglas Crowder
Typeface: VIP Palatino
Typesetter: G&S Typesetters, Inc.

Library of Congress Cataloging in Publication Data

Noggle, Burl.
  Working with history.

  Bibliography: p.
  1. Louisiana Historical Records Survey.   2. Historical
Records Survey (U.S.)   3. Louisiana—History—Sources.
4. United States—History—Sources.   I. Title.
F369.N63   976.3   81-5789
ISBN 0-8071-0881-2   AACR2

Contents

Preface

New Orleans, September, 1936: Room 302 of the courthouse at Royal and Conti Streets on the edge of the French Quarter was storage area for wills, deeds, land titles, census returns, and other legal records of life since 1803 in Louisiana. Lawyers pursuing their trade showed up from time to time in Room 302 and burrowed with distaste into the dust, the mildew, the inert (and sometimes animate) moths and roaches soiling and inhabiting the crowded cabinets that in turn crowded the large room. One attorney, who arrived in a fresh white linen suit, white shirt, and stylish tie, worked until noon, when a friend came by to suggest lunch. "Lunch, hell," muttered the attorney, "I'm going home and take a bath and change. Next time I come down here I'm going to bring a porter."

If the lawyer returned months later, he could have safely worn his southern white attire and done without the services of his (presumably black) porter. For by then, white-collar workers of the Historical Records Survey, who to one observer looked "more like ditch diggers than white-collar workers," had cleaned up the place and sorted and refiled the records, and the HRS had done a detailed inventory of the great pile of material that had accumulated over the 133 years since Thomas Jefferson bought Louisiana from Napoleon.

The Historical Records Survey had branches in every state in the late 1930s, but some state offices were more creative and productive than others. The Louisiana HRS was one of the best. To demonstrate this, and to arrive at other judgments about the entire HRS, I have examined the work of the survey in Louisiana in detail, while making periodic comparisons with surveys in other states and frequent references to the Washington office where the HRS originated and from which the Louisiana and other state offices were administered.

The HRS was a creation of the New Deal, more specifically of the Works Progress Administration, the New Deal's great experiment to provide jobs for the jobless in the Great Depression of the 1930s. Most WPA jobs were pick-and-shovel operations that demanded labor, skilled and unskilled, to build public facilities such as streets, schools, and sewage disposal plants. But through its Four Arts Program the WPA also tried to create jobs appropriate for scholars and artists. The HRS was a part of the Four Arts Program; it put people (including a few historians) to work doing things of benefit to historians—and to lawyers and other professionals as well. Given this relationship of the HRS to the New Deal and to the history profession in the United States, I have tried, essentially, to do two things with my narrative: offer a case study of a New Deal relief program in action and, at the same time, suggest a state of mind toward the profession of history that was manifested in the 1930s by the historians and other citizens who helped to create and operate the Historical Records Survey.

Finally, in an appendix I have reproduced some of the material first published by the Louisiana HRS itself in 1939. I have done this for two reasons. First, I want to go beyond my own essay—which, of course, describes and appraises the HRS inventories—and show the reader what an inventory actually looked like, from title page to table of contents to introductory essays to the inventory entries themselves. In the second place, I think some of the HRS material is worth reading, even now, some forty years after it first appeared. If the inventory entries themselves—the countless lists of what records are found on what shelf of what depository—are now sadly out of date (and were sadly neglected during a time when they could have been used), other items in the inventories are as worthwhile as they ever were. For each inventory that they published, HRS personnel wrote introductory essays on the history of the county they were surveying and on the creation and evolution of county offices such as that of sheriff. These essays, the nearest thing to history that the HRS ever produced, are often solid and informative works of historical scholarship, and they focus on a subject that historians have by and large neglected, the history of county America. The HRS in the 1930s paid more attention to the history of more American counties than historians have ever paid, before or since then. The hundreds of essays on hundreds of counties that the HRS produced are worthy of republication and reconsideration. In lieu of such a compilation, I have offered at least a sample—the essays on Saint Bernard Parish that the Louisiana HRS staff published in 1938. For comparable essays on most of the other parishes (counties) in Louisiana and many of the 3,066 counties in the nation, I recommend perusal of the HRS inventories. They are available throughout the country in the major libraries where the HRS placed them before World War II—that is, unless they have been stored away or thrown away to make room for volumes receiving more use than the neglected HRS material has enjoyed in the forty years since it first appeared in print.

WORKING WITH HISTORY

I. *Inception*

Like many other New Deal laws, agencies, and programs, the Historical Records Survey was part innovation, part consummation. The HRS, established in the midst of the Great Depression, was principally the idea of Luther H. Evans, who became its first director. Without the Depression and without Evans, the HRS would probably never have taken form. The Depression, and the effort to overcome it, brought forth the New Deal and its public works programs, one of which was the Works Progress Administration. Then, in a remarkably single-minded and energetic display of administrative acumen, Luther Evans drew up plans for the HRS and sold them to the WPA.[1] Yet the ideas, techniques, and purposes that Evans expressed or implemented had, in one form or another, been circulating among American historians and archivists for a generation.

The HRS first appeared as an agency within the Federal Writers' Project established by the Works Progress Administration in 1935. The FWP and the Federal Theatre, the Federal Music Project, and the Federal Art Project—collectively called the Four Arts Program—were labeled "Federal One" since they were the first of six federal projects

---

1. For Luther Evans' own statements about the origins of the HRS, see his essay, "The Historical Records Survey," in A. F. Kuhlman (ed.), *Public Documents* (Chicago: American Library Association, 1936), 209–214, and Evans, "The Historical Records Survey: A Statement on Its Program . . . Presented to the Sub-Committee of the Senate Committee on Education and Labor . . ." (mimeographed and circulated by the HRS, copy in Historical Records Survey Papers, Louisiana State University Archives, hereinafter cited as LHRS). An authoritative secondary account is William F. McDonald, *Federal Relief Administration and the Arts* (Columbus: Ohio State University Press, 1969), 759ff. A useful essay is David L. Smiley, "A Slice of Life in Depression America: The Records of the Historical Records Survey," *Prologue*, III (Winter, 1971), 153–59.

created within the WPA's Division of Professional and Service Projects.[2] The Federal Writers' Project was basically a relief agency designed to provide jobs and income for unemployed writers, though among FWP personnel the "writers" ranged from literary artists such as Conrad Aiken and Vardis Fisher, to typists and secretaries, to clerks whose sole qualification as writer was that they could literally write—with a pencil applied to paper—though with little felicity and little regard for syntax or even spelling.

If not everyone who worked for the FWP was a writer, neither was everyone employed by the HRS a historian, except by the most generous and casual definition. But when HRS director Luther Evans, in the summer and fall of 1935, drew up plans for the agency, gave it a rationale, and (in November, 1936) gained for it separate status from the FWP, he received much advice from several historians who were trying to do what historians had talked about doing since the turn of the century: find, salvage, protect, inventory, and make use of the public records of state and local government throughout the United States. It was Evans' particular genius to carry on this tradition by creating, in the calamity of the Depression, an agency that put to work an army of researchers who found and inventoried more records in more public archives than historians had ever thought existed.

In 1899 at its annual meeting held in Boston, the American Historical Association established a Public Archives Commission (PAC). In the stiff and careful prose characteristic of the historical profession then, the AHA "charged" the new commission "to investigate and report, from the point of view of historical study, upon the character,

2. The other projects were the Historic Building Survey, the Staffing of State Planning Boards, the Survey of Federal Archives, the Inspection of Plumbing Installations, and the Historic American Merchant Marine Survey. For the administrative history of all four arts projects, see McDonald, *Federal Relief and the Arts*. Jerre Mangione, *The Dream and the Deal: The Federal Writers' Project, 1935–1943* (Boston: Little, Brown, 1972), is lively and brimful of anecdotes, personality profiles, and shrewd observations by a participant. The best study by far of its subject is Jane DeHart Mathews, *The Federal Theatre, 1935–1939: Plays, Relief, and Politics* (Princeton: Princeton University Press, 1967). On artists, see Francis V. O'Conner (ed.), *Art for the Millions: Essays from the 1930's by Artists and Administrators of the WPA Federal Art Project* (Boston: New York Graphic Society, 1975), and Richard McKinzie, *The New Deal for Artists* (Princeton: Princeton University Press, 1973). Among copious periodical items, a recent and insightful one is Jane DeHart Mathews, "Arts and the People: The New Deal Quest for a Cultural Democracy," *Journal of American History*, LXII (September, 1975), 316–39.

contents, and functions of our public repositories of manuscript records." The commission could "appoint local agents in each state, through whom their inquiries may be in part conducted." For "organization expenses," the PAC received one hundred dollars from the parent AHA.[3]

During the next thirty-five years, the roster of the PAC, including those "local agents" it appointed, listed some of the most respected and productive names in American historiography, such as James Harvey Robinson, Herbert Levi Osgood, Charles M. Andrews, Carl Becker, U. B. Phillips, Solon Buck, Allen Johnson, and in the 1930s a gifted historian at Western Reserve University, Robert C. Binkley, who was an important link between the PAC and the new Historical Records Survey.

After its first year of operation, during which time it had collected information on archival holdings around the country, the PAC came to a gloomy conclusion: "It may be doubted if in any country in the world archives of relatively so much value are so lightly regarded or so carelessly kept." A "more rational and scientific treatment of documentary material" was an "imperative necessity," but the PAC was reluctant at the moment to propose any archival plan "with nationwide application." Instead, the commission chose to begin eliciting reports on state archives and to lend active support to any plan or program to create "state record commissions, state archivists, and the like."[4]

At the turn of the century, Massachusetts had done more than any other state to preserve and utilize its public records. In 1889 that state's legislature had created a Public Records Commission to supervise records of counties, towns, and cities. Until then, custody of town records often lay with the town clerk, who also might run a country store. Licensed to sell gunpowder, he would also stock kerosene, alcohol, excelsior, and straw. Packed away near or amidst these combustibles were the community's ancient records. The state law of 1889

3. *Annual Report of the American Historical Association for the Year 1899* (2 vols.; Washington: U.S. Government Printing Office, 1900), I, 24–25, hereinafter cited as *AHA Annual* with year; Victor Hugo Paltsits, "An Historical Resume of the Public Archives Commission," in *AHA Annual*, 1922, I, 152.

4. Paltsits, "An Historical Resume," 153.

required better protection of documents—new buildings, vaults, and safes—and transcription of decaying records and better printing and binding for current public documents.[5]

These conditions and the success of the Massachusetts public archives commission in remedying them are comparable to the work of the HRS three decades later. The HRS would discover great storehouses of documents in incredible conditions of filth and decay. And the rescue work by the HRS, though enormously larger in scope and funding, would be in essence the same as that carried on by archivists in Massachusetts and elsewhere from the turn of the century until the Depression.

Massachusetts was one of only two states (Rhode Island was the other) to establish a public archives commission by 1900. These two states were not the only ones to have neglected or lost the records of their history, however. In 1901 Herbert Levi Osgood reported to the American Historical Association on archival holdings in New York. In Onondaga county only three towns had town halls. In the county's other communities, older records were stored "wherever and however convenience dictates." Two towns had "deliberately burned their old material." In "county districts" of the state Osgood found records in stores, factories, halls, and barber shops. Some were stored in packing boxes, some in desks, and some on shelves.[6]

In character for the American historian at the turn of the century who was preoccupied with political "institutions," Osgood laid down some principles and some recommendations. He assumed that "intelligent" persons would agree on the need to preserve local records and make them accessible to users. All such local records should remain "in the custody of the officials in whose offices they originated." Still, the only way to achieve proper care of local archives was through a state records commission, one with enough power and money to control and direct town and county clerks in charge of local records. Records needed to be copied and bound, preserved in fireproof buildings and vaults, and made available to "all properly accredited persons."[7]

5. Robert T. Swan, "The Massachusetts Public Records Commission and Its Work," in *AHA Annual*, 1901, I, 97–112.
6. "Report of the Public Archives Commission," in *AHA Annual*, 1900, II.
7. *Ibid*.

The conditions Osgood described—matched by many other states —would have improved if Osgood's recommendations had become policy. Between 1900 and 1918 the PAC did nudge states a step or two toward archival reform, but in New York and elsewhere such a policy would develop only under the HRS. After 1901 the PAC surveyed archives state by state, publicized the occasional laws passed to establish archival commissions, and published several inventories and bibliographies to encourage collection, safekeeping, and use of public archives. In 1905 Arkansas created a History Commission designed to locate and preserve "all extant sources of information concerning the history of Arkansas." The Arkansas commission had begun a search for manuscripts and documents in "official depositories" outside and inside the state, extending backward to "aboriginal and Indian remains." Other states established comparable agencies. Delaware in 1905 set up a Division of Public Records. South Carolina in 1905 reorganized an historical commission created in 1894. West Virginia in 1905 established a bureau of history and archives. Maryland in 1909 authorized the land office commissioner to transcribe and rebind records in his office that needed such repair. Massachusetts, Virginia, and Louisiana passed laws to preserve and publish state records from the Civil War.[8]

Meantime, the PAC itself began to publish bibliographical items, such as a list of "Acts and Journals of the Councils and Assemblies of the Thirteen Colonies in America," compiled from colonial papers in the Public Records Office, London, by Charles M. Andrews and colleagues working under his supervision. In 1908 the PAC published reports on archives in Maine, Missouri, and Washington State that were strikingly similar to HRS reports in the 1930s: a list of offices of state government, a description of the design and facilities of each, a comment on the condition of each office's records, and a one- to two-page history of each office and of the county in which it functioned.[9] In Maine, for example, Allen Johnson found that the adjutant general's office had taken possession of a closet in the room assigned to

8. *AHA Annual*, 1905, I, 331ff., and 1909, I, 253–509. See also Herman Ames (comp.), "Resume of Archives Situations in the Several States in 1907," in *AHA Annual*, 1907, I, 159–87.

9. *AHA Annual*, 1909, I, 253–509.

the commissioner of pharmacy and was storing records there. The secretary of state's office was dumping older volumes in the basement, where they were moldering away.

Between its organization in 1899 and its near extinction in 1918, the PAC elicited and published reports (ranging from substantial to fragmentary) on archives in some forty states, among them one on Kansas' archives by Carl L. Becker, on Georgia's by U. B. Phillips, on Colorado's by Frederic L. Paxson, and on Wisconsin's by Carl Russell Fish. These were—or would later be—illustrious names in the young history profession, and their work suggests the profession's widespread interest in finding and using public documents. But despite creation of a PAC within the community of scholars that the AHA represented, the chore of finding and preserving and using public records was carried out by solitary scholars, who worked, usually without financial support, in whatever state they happened to live or happened to be concerned with in their own research. What they lacked was what the Depression crisis and the New Deal would finally give them—a patron that could organize and rationalize and help to finance a comprehensive and systematic search for public records in every office in every county in the nation. That earlier national crisis, World War I, mobilized historians to practice their trade in various ways, most of them baleful, but it seemed to have little direct effect on the PAC or the profession's request for historical records of the states currently fighting Mr. Wilson's war. In fact, by 1918 the PAC was, in its own words, "in a state of suspended activity," unable to get money for the most routine operation. The PAC finally revived in 1923, if a $100 grant from the AHA can be taken as evidence of renewal. Through the 1920s the PAC continued to proselytize for and to publish archival surveys of various states. In 1929, when he became chairman of the PAC, Charles W. Ramsdell of the University of Texas suggested that perhaps a $350 appropriation from the AHA "would not be extravagant." When Ramsdell showed up for his first PAC meeting, he found one other member there, had trouble finding out just what his committee should do, and was soon "at a loss how to proceed." He finally decided to continue the state surveys but found such a "multiplication of archival records" and such variety in their "arrangement and housing" that he despaired of doing the job with his meager funds.[10]

In 1932 Albert Ray Newsome of the University of North Carolina became chairman of the PAC. For two years he and the committee tried to complete the survey of state archives carried on between 1900 and 1918. At the same time he recognized that the old prewar surveys were now "antiquated" because of expansion in the scope and number of state government agencies. In 1934 Newsome's PAC report and one by Francis Philbrick, who was a law professor at the University of Pennsylvania and secretary of the American Legal History Society, came before the AHA executive council. Both reports called attention to recent efforts by the Social Science Research Council and the American Council of Learned Societies to organize a nationwide survey of state and local archives. The AHA council asked Newsome and Philbrick to draw up plans for a survey that "might be the basis for an appeal to the foundations."[11]

After nearly two years of New Deal public spending programs, the AHA council was still looking for support from "foundations." But learned societies other than the AHA had begun to glimpse the possibilities of New Deal programs for historians and other white-collar workers with aptitude for historical research. In fact, by April, 1934, federal relief agencies had already given substantial help to historians: thirty-two workers on a Civil Works Administration project in Colorado catalogued pamphlets and manuscripts, indexed newspapers, and interviewed pioneers; ninety-six workers in Minnesota did comparable chores, as did CWA workers in Wisconsin, Kansas, and other Midwestern states. The Alabama Department of Archives and History used aid from the Reconstruction Finance Corporation to file newspaper clippings, copy epitaphs, transcribe diaries, and carry on other archival work. Also in 1934, the Federal Emergency Relief

10. George T. Blakey, *Historians on the Homefront: American Propagandists for the Great War* (Lexington: University Press of Kentucky, 1970); Carol S. Gruber, *Mars and Minerva: World War I and the Uses of Higher Learning in America* (Baton Rouge: Louisiana State University Press, 1975); and Harold Josephson, "History for Victory: The National Board for Historical Service," *Mid-America*, LII (July, 1970), 205–224; *AHA Annual*, 1930, I, 60, 1931, I, 59–60.
11. *AHA Annual*, 1932; 1935, I, 77.

Administration tried to set up a "Program of Historical and Archival Projects." The agency invited local and state relief administrators to propose relief projects that could employ "non-manual and professional workers, teachers, and . . . librarians." The FERA suggested four historical and archival projects that state and local administrators might create: a survey of state, county, and municipal archives; classification and physical renovation of these records; survey of military records; and survey of "historical and literary manuscripts." The FERA's rationale for such projects was an echo of what historians and archivists had been saying since 1900 and was a prescient version of Luther Evans' own thinking in 1936 when he drew up plans for the HRS. The FERA maintained that its proposed surveys would produce "useful results not otherwise likely of achievement," that is, jobs for thousands of professional workers who could salvage, preserve, and make available to public officials and scholars the historical records of the nation's life. The FERA, as a matter of policy, did not envision setting up historical projects "on a national scale." Instead, all projects must derive from local and state initiative and must have a state or local sponsor, such as a university or state official. The FERA itself would pay the costs, and the Historical Division of the National Park Service would act as general coordinator of the proposed programs.[12]

In January, 1934, Francis Philbrick at the University of Pennsylvania tried to capitalize on this concern that New Dealers were showing for the nation's historical profession. Philbrick proposed to the AHA that it ask for a nationwide archival survey with "relief labor" furnished by the CWA. Philbrick also contacted Robert C. Binkley, historian at Western Reserve University, who was chairman of a Joint Committee on Materials for Research, created by the American Council of Learned Societies and the Social Science Research Council. The Joint Committee was organized, as Binkley put it, "in an effort to get maximum results for American scholarship and education from the use of relief labor." Binkley had already begun to think about federal support for

12. Theodore C. Blegen, "Some Aspects of Historical Work Under the New Deal," *Mississippi Valley Historical Review*, XXI (September, 1934), 195–206; J. Evetts Haley, memorandum on the Texas Historical Survey, "Extract from Report of the Director of the Alabama State Department of Archives and History . . . 1934" (copy of each in 43-12), "A Program of Historical and Archival Projects Under F.E.R.A.," (FERA memorandum in 43-11), all in LHRS.

surveys of state and local archives, carried out by an army of white-collar workers under supervision of trained historians. Unemployed white-collar workers, or "clerks" as he called them, were men and women who, like the clerics or clergy of Medieval Europe, worked not with tools, but with records and with people. These clerks were ideally suited for archival surveys. They could inventory records, extract information from them, copy and consolidate figures, and file and rearrange archival holdings. Binkley felt that the records most in need of such scrutiny were those of local government. Local history, local geography, and local economic studies had been neglected by social scientists, whose interest had always been in things "national." Americans had been "one of the most backward peoples of the world in the organization of localized information. New York is not only behind London, Paris, and Berlin—it is behind Prague and Budapest." Binkley would use federal relief programs to put clerks to work in the public archives and newspaper files of each American community. They should first "rescue physically the records in which alone the account of the life of the community is contained." They could then inventory, arrange, preserve, and publish the records, or otherwise make them available to scholars, lawyers, and other interested American citizens.[13]

This perspective on clerks and local archives, whereby professional scholars would train and direct mass labor to do scholarly work and the national government would coordinate work in and about localities, was not uniquely Binkley's. However, he was, perhaps, its most articulate and persuasive advocate by the early 1930s, and he circulated his ideas in a series of conferences held in Washington in 1934 and 1935. Binkley, Theodore R. Schellenberg of the National Archives, Verne E. Chatelain of the National Park Service, members of the PAC, and committees of the ACLS and the SSRC were all beginning to coalesce and bring into focus a rationale for what would become the HRS. In December, 1935, the PAC became a subcommittee of a new Committee on Historical Source Materials, and Binkley joined Newsome and Philbrick on the new subcommittee.[14] They began to

13. Robert C. Binkley, "The Cultural Program of the W.P.A.," *Harvard Educational Review*, IX (March, 1939), 156–74.
14. *AHA Annual*, 1935, 52ff. On Binkley see Max H. Fisch (ed.), *Selected Papers of*

meet in frequent consultations with Luther Evans, who, on October 1, 1935, had been named supervisor of historic projects in the WPA Four Arts program.

Evans came by his appointment in a fortuitous way. Born and raised in Bastrop County, Texas, Evans earned a B.A. degree from the University of Texas in 1924 and an M.A. there a year later. In 1927 he received a Ph.D in political science at Princeton. After teaching one year at New York University and two years at Dartmouth, Evans, in 1930, became assistant professor of political science at Princeton. In 1935 his teaching contract was not renewed for the coming academic year. Evans, who, according to rumor, lost his job because of involvement in state politics (as a Socialist), promptly sought involvement in a higher (Democratic) political realm. In June, 1935, WPA administrator Harry Hopkins discussed possibilities of a national archival survey with Raymond Moley, an early member of President Roosevelt's Brain Trust. Afterwards, Moley, who had become acquainted with Evans through one of his students at Princeton, suggested that Evans go to Washington and talk with Hopkins. Evans did, and by the end of June he was on the WPA payroll.[15]

Before June, 1935, Evans evidently knew nothing of past archival surveys or of the various current proposals for launching them. Once hired by the WPA, he promptly sought out information and advice from the best of sources. From Hopkins himself Evans learned about the tentative and uncoordinated efforts by the FERA and CWA to inventory and index local records; Hopkins, as Evans later expressed it, hoped for a "greater uniformity of purpose and method" under a national program administered by the WPA. From the American Council of Learned Societies and the Social Science Research Council, Ev-

---

Robert C. Binkley, foreword by Luther H. Evans (Cambridge: Harvard University Press, 1948), Herbert Keller, "The Historian and Life," *Mississippi Valley Historical Review*, XXIV (June, 1947), 3–36, and Perry D. Morrison, "Everyman's Archive: Robert C. Binkley and the Historical Records Survey," *The Call Number*, XVIII (Spring, 1957), 4–9.

15. William J. Sittig, "Luther Evans: Man for a New Age," *Quarterly Journal of the Library of Congress*, XXXIII (July, 1976) 251–67; Verner Clapp, "Luther H. Evans," *Library Journal*, XC (September, 1965), 3384–391; Luther Evans, "Report of Progress on the Historical Records Survey to June 30, 1936," in Historical Records Survey, Box 212, Record Group 69 (Works Progress Administration), National Archives, hereinafter cited as NA/HRS.

ans learned about the plan by their joint committee to gain CWA support for a nationwide inventory of local archival material. From Robert Binkley at Western Reserve, Francis Philbrick at the University of Pennsylvania, T. R. Schellenberg of the National Archives, Verne E. Chatelain of the National Park Service, and many other individuals and groups, Evans received a "great variety of suggestions . . . concerning the organization and methods to be utilized in setting up the project." He reduced these to what he considered "a consistent whole." By September, 1935, he had completed plans for the HRS. The WPA would sponsor the survey, which would be set up under the Federal Writers' Project, since the FWP already had a nationwide organization and seemed—at that date—to be "very similar in character" to the HRS. In November, President Roosevelt allocated initial funds of $1,195,800 to the HRS.[16] Evans was in business.

In September, Evans had proposed separating the HRS from the FWP, and by late November, 1936, he had achieved the separation. Although both of these WPA agencies were concerned with writing, the FWP, in the view of its director Henry Alsberg, "aimed at creative interpretation of American life." As it turned out, the great achievement of the FWP, apart from whatever relief and encouragement it provided to a few young creative writers who later went on to better things, was its *American Guide* series. This was less than *belles lettres* but perhaps was more "creative" than the work of the HRS, which was concerned above all with finding what Robert Binkley had called clerks to unearth, salvage, inventory, index, and sometimes publish samplings of state and local archives. As a guide for each state unit to follow in carrying out its work, Evans drew up a *Manual of the Survey of Historical Records*, which described how to set up a field organization and which contained samples of forms that workers were to use in compiling archival information. Evans sent to all HRS state supervisors a completed sample guide to the Muskogee County, Oklahoma, archives. According to this sample, guides to county archives were to contain an historical sketch of the county, an outline of its

16. Evans, "The HRS," in *Public Documents*; Evans, "Report of Progress on the HRS." McDonald, *Federal Relief and the Arts*, 751–57, is a concise account of this and other historical projects established or proposed under FERA and CWA auspices.

governmental organization, a description of all county offices, a listing of all their records, and a description of their housing, care, organization, and accessibility.[17]

In early January, 1936, Evans, working at first through the FWP, took the final step that brought into being the HRS he had begun to formulate in June, 1935. He created an HRS office in each state and put historians and archivists and other clerks to work. And thereby the HRS came to Louisiana.

17. McDonald, *Federal Relief and the Arts*, 761ff, 763; *AHA Annual*, 1936, p. 53.

II. *Underway (More or Less)*

In each state the state director of the Federal Writers' Project was to become state supervisor of the Historical Records Survey. In Louisiana this was Lyle Saxon, who had taken charge of the Louisiana Writers' Project in October, 1935, and who became one of the best state directors the FWP ever had. Saxon was reluctant to maintain for long the administrative fusion whereby the state Writers' Project and the state HRS had the same director and seemed at times to be doing comparable, if not the same, chores. In January, 1936, however, Evans (through the office of FWP director Henry Alsberg) offered Saxon the job of HRS supervisor, and Saxon accepted it. Saxon and Evans also set out to find an assistant state supervisor who would have "principal responsibility" for the HRS in the state. Already, in November, 1935, Evans had contacted Edwin A. Davis, historian at Louisiana State University, asking Davis for information on archives in Louisiana and offering Davis the job as HRS director in the state.[1]

Davis was an appropriate contact. In October, 1934, when the FERA had tried to begin a survey of local archives in Louisiana, librarians and historians at Tulane and LSU had agreed that Davis was "the logical man" to plan and carry out the survey. Davis, with energy and acumen, drew up his ambitious "Plan for a Louisiana State Historical Survey" that would employ some 200 workers in twelve districts in the

1. Ronnie W. Clayton, "A History of the Federal Writers' Project in Louisiana" (Ph.D. dissertation, Louisiana State University, 1974), 37; Henry Alsberg to Lyle Saxon, January 4, 1935, in Box 258, Record Group No. 69 (Work Projects Administration), National Archives, hereinafter cited ad NA/HRS; Luther Evans to Edwin Davis, November 22, 1935, in HRS Papers, Department of Archives, Louisiana State University Library, Baton Rouge, hereinafter cited as LHRS.

state and would spend about $84,000 in the "three to four months" that Davis thought it would take to complete the survey. Davis modeled his plan after the "General Instructions on the Making of Inventory Lists of Manuscripts and Manuscripts Collections" that the National Park Service sent to him. At this stage in the history of the HRS—after Evans had begun to design it but before it had finally taken form—the National Park Service was still helping to initiate and administer archival surveys carried on by New Deal relief programs. Davis also sought advice from Thomas Owen of Alabama and J. Evetts Haley of Texas, each of whom had set up CWA historical surveys in his state.[2] Davis' survey never materialized, but his name and his obvious proclivity for archival work became known to T. R. Schellenberg and other archivists in Washington, who passed the word on to Evans.

Davis rejected the offer to become Director of the HRS in Louisiana, but, from his position as archivist at LSU, he would become a prominent and crucial patron and adviser to the men who did direct the Survey during its six years of existence in the state. The first of these directors was Dr. Gaspar Lugano, who became project supervisor early in 1936 with an office in the Canal Bank in New Orleans. Lugano, a doctor of jurisprudence (Royal University of Pavia, Italy), was a linguist who knew Greek, Latin, Italian, French, and Spanish. Fluency in the last two languages was perhaps Lugano's chief qualification for his job. Although he was the nominal director of the Louisiana HRS and was directly responsible to Louisiana Writers' Project director Lyle Saxon, Lugano was not listed as assistant state supervisor. In all other states (except Oregon and South Dakota), the state director of the HRS bore such a title, but neither Evans nor Saxon was quite satisfied with the choice they had to make in 1936. Evans had wanted Davis, and offered him the job again in October. Saxon wanted to separate the HRS from the LWP. Only with that separation and the appointment of John Andreassen as director of the state HRS in March,

2. Robert J. Usher to Davis, October 15, 1934, Usher to James A. McMillen, November 5, 1934, Ronald F. Lee (Acting Chief Historian, NPS) to Davis, December 3, 1934, Thomas Owen to Davis, December 6, 1934, J. Evetts Haley to Davis, December 3, 1934, all in 43-11, LHRS.

1937, did Louisiana begin to rise to prominence, if not preeminence, among the HRS units in the nation.[3]

When he selected Lugano as project supervisor, Saxon also began appointing the twenty-five workers that Evans allotted to Louisiana. Sixteen of these would work in the New Orleans office—this in keeping with Evans' instructions that Saxon "in the beginning" restrict the survey to the historic old city. Evans made a first allotment of $12,868.13 to Louisiana, releasing 75 percent of this amount ($9,650.00) in January and agreeing to release the remainder in four months. Evans determined the funds for each state on the basis of population and then made adjustments according to the availability of white-collar relief labor, of competent supervisors, and of local projects already underway.[4] When Evans released to Louisiana 75 percent of its original allotment, he was simply following the formula he used for all states. It remained for Saxon and Lugano to demonstrate their need for more funds by making effective use of the $9,650 Evans granted them.

The Louisiana HRS was one of the first state units to get underway, but it sputtered for weeks before it began to function to Evans' satisfaction. Such a performance was common among the new HRS units in operation by March, 1936. Evans had created five regions of the HRS, placing Louisiana in Region III, along with Alabama, Arkansas, Florida, Georgia, Mississippi, North Carolina, Oklahoma, South Carolina, Tennessee, Texas, and Virginia. Region I contained the six New England states, plus the New York State and the New York City surveys, the latter counting as a state in Evans' table of organization. Region II included Delaware, Maryland, New Jersey, Pennsylvania, West Virginia, and the District of Columbia. Region IV was made up of Illinois, Indiana, Iowa, Kansas, Kentucky, Michigan, Minnesota, Missouri, Nebraska, North Dakota, Ohio, South Dakota, and Wisconsin. Region V encompassed Arizona, California, Colorado, Idaho, Montana, Nevada, New Mexico, Oregon, Utah, Washington, and Wyo-

3. Evans to Harry Hopkins, February 29, 1936, in Progress Reports, Box 212, Saxon to Evans, March 4, April 23, 1936, in General Correspondence, Box 43, both in NA/HRS; Davis to Evans, October 23, 1936, in 43-11, LHRS.

4. Evans to Saxon, January 31, 1926, in Gen. Corr., Box 43, Evans, "Progress Reports" (mimeograph copies in Prog. Rpts., Box 212), both in NA/HRS.

ming. The five-region pattern reflected traditional thinking. Region III, for example, was obviously "the South," though Kentucky was left out and Texas and Oklahoma were debatably more western than southern. Evans also drew on newer concepts of regionalism current in the 1930s.[5] He created no regional offices, but by March 1, 1936, he had set up HRS offices in twenty states as well as in New York City and the District of Columbia, an office separate from his own National Coordinating Office. Soon he would establish units in the remaining twenty-eight states. In mid-February he drew up the first of the series of great reports that he would submit to his administrative superiors in the WPA in the next four years. He ranged from praise to concern, from admiration to scorn, as he moved in alphabetical order through the list of states.

Alabama, for instance, had given him "certain difficulties," since the state's Department of Archives and History had already used Reconstruction Finance Corporation and Civil Works Administration funds to compile records—especially genealogies—but was "not strong on inventory work" and at first was "somewhat hostile" to Evans' plans to launch a more comprehensive program. In Arizona the HRS director was reportedly trying "to make a political football of appointments." Colorado seemed ready to do "a very satisfactory inventory" since several competent historians (among them George L. Anderson of Colorado College and Leroy Hafen of the state historical society) had done county inventories under FERA auspices and were eager to extend them with HRS help. Florida had become a "serious problem." The state librarian, in charge of a survey already underway, was proving uncooperative, and the state HRS supervisor had "her mind set on translating and copying records"—something Evans, at the time, did not want done. In Kentucky, Evans had the "welcome services" of historian Thomas D. Clark, who was "very successful and progressive in his ideas about inventory work." HRS work in Massachusetts was "further advanced . . . than in any other state," partly because of the enterprise of historian Clifford Shipton, director

5. On the concept of regionalism, see Vernon Carstensen, "The Development and Application of Regional-Sectional Concepts, 1900–1950," in Merrill Jensen (ed.), *Regionalism in America* (Madison: University of Wisconsin Press, 1952), 99–118; also Earl H. Rovit, "The Regions Versus the Nation: Critical Battle of the Thirties," *Mississippi Quarterly*, XIII (Spring, 1960), 90–98.

of the Massachusetts Writers' Project, who was directing the state HRS without the help of an assistant state supervisor. Michigan had caused a "few headaches" because the State Historical Commission was "heavily loaded with jealous conservatives." In contrast, neighboring Minnesota was "one of the most advanced states of the Union in manuscript and archival work," and Evans anticipated "eminently satisfactory results" in the state. In Mississippi a "difficult situation" had arisen: Dunbar Rowland, director of the Department of Archives and History, refused to "have anything whatsoever to do with" the HRS. He had made a survey of Mississippi county records in 1902 and "thinks that it is an insult to him to suggest . . . additional work." Evans decided to ignore Rowland and work directly with the head of the Mississippi Writers' Project, who had taken "a very intelligent interest" in the HRS. In New Jersey, Evans' first appointment as state supervisor turned out to be a Republican, which provoked "violent exception" from the state's WPA administrator. After some delay and "through some miracle," Evans managed to retain the appointee, a man of "unusual executive ability" who was also "well versed" in New Jersey history. In South Carolina, Evans found "people more emotionally than intellectually interested in history," and he had not yet released funds to the state. Tennessee was especially nettlesome: the director of the state writers' project was a "pseudo historian," and the state archivist did not know "the elemental facts about history and historical records." In contrast, Wisconsin was "one of the more intelligent states in the matter of historical records," and Evans had released $28,900 to operate the state project to May 15.[6]

In varying degrees of readiness, then, and under varying leadership, surveys were underway in twenty states by March 1, 1936. In June, 1936, Evans evaluated the administrators he had hired and the sponsors or advisers in each state who had volunteered their counsel to these administrators. Assistant state supervisors of the HRS he judged to be of "high caliber as regards educational background and professional standing." Twelve held Ph.D. degrees. Two of these, George P. Hammond of New Mexico and Alfred Powers of Oregon, were deans of their respective state universities. Several of the supervi-

6. Luther Evans, "Report on the Status of the HRS," February, 1936 (mimeograph copy in Prog. Rpts., Box 212, NA/HRS).

sors were already serving as state archivists, and in Virginia, Supervisor Lester J. Cappon was archivist of the state university. Four supervisors held "positions of eminence" in their state historical societies: Alice E. Smith was curator of manuscripts in Wisconsin; Edward P. Alexander was secretary in New York's society; Owen C. Coy was director of the California Historical Association; and Clarence C. Crittenden was secretary of the North Carolina Historical Commission.[7]

Louisiana's offering to this distinguished group of supervisors, most of whom were already or would soon be respected scholars, was Dr. Gaspar Lugano. If not a Ph.D. in history, he was a Doctor of Jurisprudence. If not director of the state's archives (Louisiana, in fact, had no such official agency until 1936), he had served as archivist at the Catholic cathedral in New Orleans, and both the church and the city had been of great moment in the history of the state. Nevertheless, Lyle Saxon and Evans had chosen not to give him the title of assistant state supervisor. Saxon judged him to be "by far the most intelligent and capable person that we have on our staff, but . . . not [of] executive ability to act as Supervisor." Also, this "Italian gentleman" sometimes had "difficulty in making himself understood." Saxon was referring to Lugano's accent, but this linguist's written English was often no clearer than his spoken expression. Informed one day that a conference had been postponed, he noted, "its postponement remains within the province of negligible significancy." On the other hand, Lugano and Saxon worked together better than did some administrators elsewhere. Evans reported early "friction and misunderstanding" in Illinois between the director of the state writers' project and the HRS supervisor. In Pennsylvania the writers' project director, located in Philadelphia, and Curtis W. Garrison of the HRS, headquartered in Harrisburg, "vigorously [fought] one another for complete control of the Survey." Florida offered a variaton on this kind of bickering. There the writers' project director and the HRS supervisor worked together but "engaged in war with another group of historians." One of the leaders in the "enemy camp" was the state librarian, who, in operating a state archives survey of his own, aroused "jeal-

7. Evans, "Report on the Status," June 30, 1936.

ousy and friction" between his workers and those of the Florida HRS.[8]

As the brawl in Florida demonstrates, historians did not always welcome creation of the HRS. But enthusiasm, support, and good (and free) advice were more common responses that historians offered to arrival of the Survey. In several states "advisory committees" of historians took form and volunteered to help the HRS plan and carry out its work. In New York, the chairman of the advisory committee was Alexander C. Flick, state historian, who enlisted cooperation of "most of the outstanding historians of the state," among them Dixon Ryan Fox of Union College. In Illinois an impressive list of scholars fostered the HRS, among them state archivist Margaret C. Norton; Theodore C. Pease, editor of the Illinois Historical Collection; and Herbert A. Kellar of the McCormick Historical Association. In North Carolina Albert R. Newsome, of the history department at the state university in Chapel Hill, was an active adviser to a state project that, in time, became one of the best in the South.[9]

As on most other comparative scales, Louisiana in 1936 fell somewhere between the extremes in the support it received from historians in the state. No one of them and no organized group of them ever emerged as prominent critic. The young Edwin A. Davis (who received his Ph.D. in history from LSU in 1936) appeared to be the most active HRS supporter that the state university's history department produced, at least until 1937 when John Andreassen came out of that same department to replace Lugano in the HRS. Meantime, Lyle Saxon, though himself a historian of sorts, gave time and attention to the HRS but was more anxious to get on with his guidebook and other publications of the state writers' project.[10]

Employment and production figures in the HRS were subject to objective measurement and were, therefore, more tangible and, per-

8. Saxon to Evans, April 23, 1936, Gaspar Lugano to Sargent Child, July 24, 1936, both in Gen. Corr., Box 43, Evans, "Report on the Status," May, 1936, all in NA/HRS.

9. Evans, "Report on the Status," June 30, 1936.

10. Saxon wrote several books about Louisiana, including the novel, *Children of Strangers* (Boston: Houghton Mifflin, 1937), and collections of essays: *Fabulous New Orleans* (New York: D. Appleton-Century, 1928), *Father Mississippi* (New York: Century, 1927), *Lafitte the Pirate* (New York: Century, 1930), and *Old Louisiana* (New York: Century, 1929). On Saxon as historian, see Clayton, "A History of the FWP in Louisiana," 300–334.

haps, more important than the administration of the Survey and the advice it received. How many workers did what kind of work in Louisiana and elsewhere in the first few months of the HRS? On May 1, 1936, Evans calculated that 3,774 workers were employed in the fifty-one units of the HRS (forty-eight state offices, plus one for New York City, one for the District of Columbia, and Evans' own Coordinating Office in Washington). The employee count ranged from 10 in West Virginia to 400 in New York State (and 93 more in New York City). Thirty-three were at work in Louisiana, all of them in New Orleans. Because of what Evans described as a "huge quantity of historical material" in the two cities, the Louisiana HRS worked only in New Orleans and Baton Rouge during most of 1936. The New Orleans office began active operation on March 9. By April 7, Lugano and 16 workers were on the payroll there, and by July 7, 40 more had been hired. The Baton Rouge office opened in May, with a quota of 10 workers. The quota for each city would increase in the months to come, as would appropriations.[11]

As Evans said again and again, the HRS was designed to take inventory of county, town, and other local public records. He and his staff also developed forms for workers to fill out, established procedures for them to follow, laid down standards for them and state HRS administrators to uphold. But obviously these were general guidelines. It remained for Louisiana to determine what its particular records were and how to inventory and preserve and utilize them. Even before the New Orleans HRS began operation, it was receiving information and suggestions on how to proceed. In March a young historian named Roger W. Shugg learned about the HRS from a colleague, who passed on to Evans a letter that Shugg wrote about the HRS. Evans, in turn, sent the letter to Saxon and suggested that Saxon act on it. Shugg had recently finished his Princeton dissertation, "The Rise of the Poor White in Louisiana," and was full of information and insights about Louisiana history and equally full of enthusiasm about what the HRS could do. "It goes far beyond anything I dreamed of and will be of untold value for all of us historians." Shugg wanted to "especially recommend Louisiana." The state was a "meeting-place of

11. Evans, "Report on the Status," May, 1936; Newsletter #3 (copy in State Series, Box H-M, 1935–39), and Gen. Corr., Box 43, all in NA/HRS.

French, Spanish, and American culture with valuable records dating back to 1720, but without an active State Archives department and consequently dependent upon [the HRS] for bringing order to its scattered materials." Shugg recommended several "local people" as "conversant with Louisiana records," among them historians Walter Prichard at LSU and John S. Kendall at Tulane, the librarian at Tulane and at the New Orleans public library, and Lyle Saxon. He pointed out—rightly—that the last survey of state archives, a brief report by William O. Scroggs, professor of economics and sociology at LSU, for the Public Archives Commission, had been published in 1912. Scroggs had focused on archives in New Orleans and Baton Rouge, ignoring local records in the parishes. He reported that Spanish records were abundant, though poorly protected, and that records from the French and early American periods were meager because of fires, neglect, and the fact that the capital had been moved seven times. Scroggs's survey revealed what Shugg found still true in 1936: parish and plantation records were "scattered [or] unknown." Shugg thought that a catalog of parish courthouse archives was the "most profitable and difficult work" the HRS could do. Also, the new state capitol in Baton Rouge, just completed under Huey Long's direction, stood in "great need of indexing its archives." Shugg mentioned other items and sources, such as uncatalogued pamphlets stacked "in dusty bundles" at Tulane and legislative and judicial reports at the state law library in New Orleans. All of these collections needed "inspection and notation" and could be handled "easily and quickly" by HRS workers.[12]

Shugg was too ambitious and too optimistic. He wanted the HRS to survey more than Evans had designed it to do. And the work that it did undertake was neither easily nor quickly done. Between March 9, 1936, when it began operation, and June 30, 1936, when it submitted a summary report to Evans, Lugano's crew in New Orleans surveyed 30 percent of the parish records there, a small percentage of the state records located there, and one-third of the church archives in the city.

12. Roger W. Shugg, *Origins of Class Struggle in Louisiana* (Baton Rouge: Louisiana State University Press, 1939); William O. Scroggs, "The Archives of the State of Louisiana," *Annual Report of the American Historical Association for 1912* (Washington: Government Printing Office, 1914), 275–93, hereinafter cited as *AHA Annual* with year; Shugg to Nelson R. Burr, March 6, 1936, Evans to Saxon, March, 1936, both in Gen. Corr., Box 43, NA/HRS.

In addition, Lugano reported that an "extensive painting and statuary inventory" was in progress in the city and that a "large number of manuscript collections" were being surveyed. Meantime, the Baton Rouge office, beginning work on May 18, had by June 23 made inventory of "less than 1%" of the records in East Baton Rouge Parish. Allocation for this work—vaguely defined though it was and extending beyond Evans' instructions to survey "public records"—totaled $9,309.50 as of June 6, 1936, with seven dollars allotted to New Orleans for each two dollars spent in Baton Rouge. On June 8, Evans released $1,500 more to Saxon and on July 7, an additional $3,150. By August 5, Louisiana's employment quota reached seventy-five and climbed to eighty-five on October 1. By mid-October Lugano had assigned some fifty workers to several jobs, as clerks or researchers or both. Besides the ten secretarial or clerical workers in Lugano's own editorial office, he had assigned forty more workers to various archives and administrative units around the city, sending nine to the civil district courts, two to the state Board of Health, three to the Confederate Memorial, four to the Sewerage and Water Board in City Hall, and six to the Commissioner's Office of the Port of New Orleans. By November Lugano and his staff had inventoried seventy-nine agencies in New Orleans, ranging from the Attorney's Office in City Hall, to the Fire Department, to the Night Recorder's Court. And by this date Lugano had begun to send a few workers into neighboring parishes (two to Saint John the Baptist and three to Saint Charles).[13]

The first item that Lugano offered to Evans for approval and possible publication was the "Inventory of Court Records. State of Louisiana." Despite its title, it covered only Orleans Parish and the city of New Orleans. Even before Lugano submitted it, he was reminded that it did not conform to Evans' directive to focus on county (parish) records. Sargent Child, who in 1936 was a field supervisor and who later would succeed Evans as director of the HRS, visited New Orleans in September. Child was perplexed to find Lugano at work on

---

13. Newsletter #3; Saxon to Evans, June 6, 1936, Sargent Child to Saxon, June 7, 1936, Lugano to Evans, September 1, 1936, Ellen S. Woodward to James H. Crutcher, September 30, 1936, Evans to Saxon, September 30, 1936, Lugano to Evans, October 9, 22, 1936, Lugano to Evans, December 2, 31, 1936, all in Gen. Corr., Box 43, NA/HRS.

court records. When Lugano sent the inventory to Washington for approval, he also wrote Evans a long letter trying to justify what he had done. He had, he argued, encountered "[political] obstacles in all directions" when he tried to inventory parish records. Local political figures had discouraged him, even denied him access to local depositories. In contrast, he had found "ready comprehension and . . . assistance" from the judiciary. But it was not merely "expedient" to work on judicial records. In defense of his work, Lugano, the linguist, delivered to Evans, political scientist, a long discourse on the importance of the judiciary in American life.[14]

Evans approved publication of the inventory, subject to some editorial corrections and condensation. Meantime, through the remainder of 1936, Lugano's staff in New Orleans continued to work in other directions—sometimes within, sometimes beyond the guidelines Evans had drawn. Besides poking around in churches and cemeteries looking for "historical data" and vital statistics, Lugano's group also gathered records on eighty-three municipal depositories in New Orleans. And finally moving out of the city and into neighboring parishes, they began work on what would prove to be a seminal and heralded publication, the *St. Charles Parish Inventory*.[15]

During 1936, while the Lugano group in New Orleans gradually organized and finally began to produce acceptable inventories, the HRS office in Baton Rouge, which began work later and hired fewer workers, found more records and eventually conformed more to Evans' standards of what to inventory, in what way, than did Lugano's crew in New Orleans. But during its first few weeks of operation, the Baton Rouge project was "confusion manifested," as one supervisor later reported. On May 1, eight employees (ten were authorized) went to work in the Baton Rouge office under direction of Marguerite Ellis, who supervised the East Baton Rouge Parish HRS as well as the American Guide Project launched there by Saxon's LWP. Three months later, on July 27, Irene C. Wagner assumed duty as HRS supervisor in the city, relieving Ellis of her double duty. When Wagner took over, she found twelve workers on the job. Lyle Saxon had informed her that the "status" of the Baton Rouge HRS corresponded

14. Lugano to Evans, October 14, 1936, in Gen. Corr., Box 43, NA/HRS.
15. Child to Lugano, October 27, 1936, in *ibid.*

to that of the New Orleans office; she was to report directly to Evans, not to Saxon or Lugano. In compliance, she promptly sent Evans a report on how many workers were doing what in the parish. Three were at work on parish archives in the clerk of court office; two were digging into state archives in the basement of the Old State Capitol; two were "in the field" gathering data for use in the LWP's *Louisiana Guidebook*; several others were secretaries or editors.[16]

Such a breakdown or table of organization did not—could not—suggest the confusion in the mind and the chaos in the archives that the Baton Rouge group felt and met in their first months on the job. Marvin Libby, an HRS field supervisor, spent six days in Baton Rouge early in September and reported his observations and findings to Evans. Libby found some "extenuating circumstances" for the "confusion" that Wagner herself had sensed upon her arrival on the job. It was difficult enough for a supervisor to recruit workers, train them for their chores, and establish a routine of work in parish archives; it was difficulty compounded to handle, as well, the research and writing needed to produce the *American Guides*. Also, Lugano's office, after acquiring some skill in doing their own inventories and indices, had been unable to afford some "active direction" to the Baton Rouge office when it opened. New Orleans had sent letters of instruction and sample inventories to Baton Rouge, but this was not enough. "It has been our experience," said Libby, "that very little can be accomplished in meetings or by written instructions to field workers." Only "actual inventory of . . . different types of records (bound, unbound, printed, etc.) under the direction of a trained worker [will permit] productive efforts." And it required more workers than the Baton Rouge office had to do the job at hand "to make up a list of depositories, fill out depository cards, establish a proper system of office filing, gain access to the numerous state offices, adequately train the field workers, and yet accomplish much in the way of actual inventory." And finally, Libby cited the "utter confusion of many of the state records," due in part to the confusion and transfer of political rule in Louisiana history. Baton Rouge in its time had been French,

16. Marvin Libby, "Report on East Baton Rouge Parish," September, 1936 (typescript in 43-11, LHRS). Edward Dreyer (assistant state director, LWP) to Evans, May 14, 1936, Wagner to Evans, July 31, August 15, 1936, all in Gen. Corr., Box 43, NA/HRS.

British, and Spanish, as well as American. The capital had from time to time been moved from New Orleans to Baton Rouge to Opelousas to Shreveport to New Orleans again and finally back to Baton Rouge. All these transfers of sovereignty and change in location, along with the "ravages of war and fire," had led, as Libby wryly understated it, to "some loss, spoilage, and serious disarrangement" of public archives.[17]

Libby went from office to office, archive to archive, talking to HRS workers and suggesting how they could do a better job. At the new East Baton Rouge Parish courthouse on Saint Louis Street, overlooking the Mississippi from the modest heights two blocks away from the levee, Libby found two workers taking inventory and one "straightening out a jumble of miscellaneous unbound records." The workers were doing their job, filling out inventory cards, accurately enough. But, again, as with almost every HRS project in Louisiana, the complexities and accidents of the past lay reflected in the judicial records shelved and scattered about the courthouse rooms and storage bins. The state of Louisiana, under its several state constitutions, had been redistricted several times. East Baton Rouge Parish had, at various times, been in seven judicial districts. Exact dates for each of these transfers were hard to determine. Records of the earlier courts lay stacked "at random along the top of sectioned steel shelving running the entire length of the west wall in the record room." The HRS workers taking inventory had made no effort to rearrange the records and group them according to the district or the period to which they belonged. At Libby's suggestion, and with approval from the resident custodian, Wagner's staff set out to rearrange, classify, and inventory all criminal and civil court records they found in the parish courthouse.[18]

Meantime, the HRS crew assigned to the old statehouse had stumbled into a maze of cobwebs and clutter. When Louisiana moved its seat of state government into Huey Long's gleaming new capitol, the old structure, which Mark Twain once labeled Cherokee Gothic, still housed a basement full of "worthless" records. The HRS found them "heaped en masse" ready to be burned. Wagner's crew laboriously

17. Libby, "Report on East Baton Rouge Parish," September, 1936.
18. *Ibid.*

poked through some of this seeming refuse and found things worthy of salvage. Wagner and Edwin A. Davis, who had recently become director of archives at LSU, worked out a scheme to salvage and inventory this material. Davis secured from Governor Richard Leche an executive order granting him authority to "remove all documents that he desires" from the old state capitol and store them, "properly catalogued and indexed," at LSU. Six of Wagner's HRS crew, along with several workers on loan from the National Youth Administration, salvaged and inventoried enough material to fill four rooms in the old capitol, and Davis removed selected portions of these documents to LSU.[19] By the end of the year, under Wagner's competent direction, the Baton Rouge HRS was working with efficiency, and the HRS in Louisiana was beginning to spread into other towns and parishes of the state.

19. *Ibid.*; Wagner to Evans, September 17, 1936, Wagner to Davis, October 21, 1936, W. J. Everett (secretary to Governor Leche) to Davis, October 27, 1936, all in 43-11, LHRS; Wagner to Evans, December 11, 1936, in Gen. Corr., Box 43, NA/HRS.

III. *The Best in the South*

In February, 1937, in one of his periodic reports, Luther Evans in Washington surveyed Region III of the HRS and declared his satisfaction with Lugano's office in New Orleans and Wagner's in Baton Rouge. This hardly made Louisiana unique among HRS units. Evans was "surprised to realize" that nowhere in Region III had he found "any serious administrative or technical problems." In Alabama "friction" had developed between the state writers' project and the state HRS, and the AWP director had for many months "belittled the abilities of the HRS director," but by early 1937 "the situation [had] greatly improved." In Arkansas the writers' project director had tried also to direct the HRS in the state, with disastrous results. Sargent Child, Evans' traveling field supervisor, found the state project "distinctly below the general average" and arranged appointment of a new HRS supervisor who had to "start from scratch." Recent reports from Arkansas showed "marked improvements," and Evans thought the state would "gradually catch up with the procession." In Florida a state archives survey was already at work when the state HRS began operations. In July, 1936, when the two offices merged, the earlier work of the state archives survey was so poor that, as in Arkansas, a "new beginning had to be made." But soon, work in county records "was in full blast" in almost all of Florida's sixty-seven counties. This pattern of early mistakes and incompetence, later corrected and overcome, held in Georgia. The first HRS director there, a "representative of the D.A.R. and other groups," proved to be a poor administrator. A new supervisor and several competent editors had taken "great strides forward in the past few months," and Evans had "ceased to be uneasy about Georgia." The Mississippi HRS "suffered" during its first six months of operation, but then showed "great improvement." The North Carolina HRS had knowledgeable and competent direction from the first day of operation. Dr. C. C. Crittenden, secretary and director of the North Carolina Historical Commission, became HRS supervisor on January 4, 1936, and, as Evans noted, "launched the work of the Survey immediately." Crittenden's only fault appeared to be his occasional "irritation at WPA regulations," for which trait Evans "gently rebuked him." In Oklahoma, Supervisor Robert H. Slover did an "unusually good job" all through 1936, and the Oklahoma HRS was, in Evans' view, "one of the four or five best in the entire Survey." The South Carolina office, unusual in that from the start it operated separately from the state writers' project, had become "a source of great satisfaction" to Evans. In Tennessee Evans had to replace the original HRS supervisor, Louis Kaplan, when he encountered "prejudices . . . against his race" from state WPA officials. Kaplan also suffered from "ill-advised and erratic interference" from the associate director of the Tennessee writers' project. Tennessee inventories done in 1936 were "below the general average" for Region III, but the new HRS supervisor, T. Marshall Jones, had been "carefully coached" in his duties, and the state was finally producing a few county surveys. The Texas HRS, with a large quota of workers (between 200 and 250 during the period May to September, 1936) had been handicapped by the "enormous territory to be covered" (254 counties), but the Survey's work was "of very high quality." In Virginia several historians of current or future stature worked on the HRS. The state writers' project director, H. J. Eckenrode, helped to launch the program and then delegated "complete authority" over it to Lester J. Cappon, archivist at the University of Virginia. Cappon, in turn, granted responsibility to Edwin Hemphill, his assistant at the university. Meantime, much of the HRS work done in the state was done in Richmond under direction of the district supervisor there, Elizabeth Parker. The Virginia HRS had at times lacked "sufficient vigor," but Evans had "no complaint" about it by February, 1937.[1]

1. Evans Memo, February 13, 1937 (mimeograph copy in Progress Reports, Box 212,

In comparison to these states in Region III, Louisiana was neither a laggard nor a pacesetter. Like the Survey in most other states, the Louisiana HRS still operated under administration of the writers' project. But also like most other state directors, Lyle Saxon had given Lugano and Wagner virtual autonomy over their New Orleans and Baton Rouge offices, and these two supervisors had performed as well as most state supervisors. In measurable terms of employment quotas and county (parish) surveys completed, Louisiana, as in most matters, fell closer to the median than to the outer edge of an imaginary scale of Region III surveys. Among the twelve states in the region, the Oklahoma HRS began operation in March, 1936, with the smallest number of workers—five—but by Feburary, 1937, it had sixty-three on the rolls. North Carolina began its survey with fifty workers—the largest staff then in the region—and listed seventy-one employees in February, 1937. Texas, beginning with thirty-one workers in March 1936, had hired a total of 116 by January, 1937. Louisiana, by comparison, began operation in March, 1936, with twelve workers (all in New Orleans) and listed seventy-three at work in February, 1937 (mostly in New Orleans and Baton Rouge). These Louisiana workers had, by early 1937, begun inventories in eleven of the state's sixty-four parishes and had sent five complete or partial drafts of parish inventories to Washington for Evans' perusal. This record was comparable to that of most other states in Region III. For example, by early 1937 Alabama had done work in seventeen of its sixty-seven counties, had completed surveys in six of the seventeen, and had submitted one county inventory to Evans. The North Carolina HRS had moved with alacrity into ninety-four of a hundred counties and had listed some 90 percent of the records in those counties. In Tennessee the Survey had restricted itself to eight of the state's ninety-five counties and had, by February, 1937, almost finished the inventory of those eight but had submitted only one inventory draft to Washington for approval. As in Louisiana, where Lugano had chosen to inventory judicial records as well as parish records, several states

---

Record Group No. 69 [Work Projects Administration], National Archives, hereinafter cited as NA/HRS).

in Region III had also ranged beyond county archives. Virginia had listed the records of 1,250 of its estimated 3,000 churches. The North Carolina HRS had done "considerable listing" in the manuscript collections at Duke University, The University of North Carolina, and the Presbyterian Archives at Montreat.[2]

Apart from an occasional professional in charge of a state HRS unit, such as Crittenden in North Carolina, the HRS hired few historians (like the Federal Writers' Project, which hired few writers). Under WPA regulations, the HRS had to draw at least 85 percent of its personnel from relief rolls. Evans' original scheme had been to hire personnel at a fixed ratio: three "professionals" to four "skilled" to one "unskilled" worker. This notion he had to abandon; most applicants for survey work, drawn from the relief rolls, had at best a high school education, though lack of education was not always the worker's major deficiency. J. M. Scammell, a field supervisor, reported to Evans in December, 1936, on HRS personnel in Idaho: "Here we have to deal with not only simple psychopathic cases and frustrated females but hop-heads, homos, and all sorts of screwy people whom the WPA could not get on with and who were transferred to [the HRS]." William R. Hogan, a young historian working with HRS personnel in Louisiana in 1939, reported that he had "seen and heard three Survey courthouse workers asleep in the same room, but my only emotion was gratification because I knew [they] were doing less harm in somnolence than they would be in their waking moments." Hogan also recalled seeing workers patiently gazing at manuscripts held upside down.[3]

Given the modest education and minimal experience of most HRS workers, Evans and his state supervisors had to create a procedure for them to follow, a series of inventory forms for them to fill out, and a process of supervision and editing whereby unskilled workers, seem-

2. *Ibid.*
3. Evans Memo, June 30, 1936, in Prog. Rpts., Box 212, NA/HRS; Scammell quoted in William F. McDonald, *Federal Relief Administration and the Arts* (Columbus: Ohio State University Press, 1969), 780; Hogan's full report in 43-11, HRS Papers, Department of Archives, Louisiana State University Library, Baton Rouge, hereinafter cited as LHRS. For detailed discussion of the WPA's system of working through the U.S. Employment Service, and the cumbersome scheme for classifying and assigning workers to the HRS and other agencies in Federal One, see McDonald, *Federal Relief and the Arts*, 189–202, and 777–84.

ingly fit only for manual labor or at best simple clerical chores, could do to satisfaction the work that Evans had designed the HRS to do.[4] In fact, Evans often spoke with justifiable pride about how HRS workers, following the methods he perfected, had "shown a special aptitude for accepting training in the type of work being carried forward by the Survey." The HRS, he claimed, was producing "technical work of good quality" while at the same time it "fulfilled the basic responsibility of WPA to keep workers busy at tasks which prevent[ed] the deterioration of their morale and their skill." Even if any unskilled laborer thereby became a semiskilled clerk, however, he received at best a modest salary. In December, 1936, Lugano reported that the average wage in the Louisiana HRS was $77.50 per month. This sum almost precisely matched the Survey's national average, which was $77 in June, 1936. As of June, about 30 percent of HRS personnel were women, although the percentage was much higher in a few states (70 percent in Florida, South Carolina, and Alabama). Evans noted the HRS made "no sex distinction in salaries." It did, of course, make a distinction in salaries paid to Survey supervisors. In the summer of 1936, when the average HRS worker was making $77 a month, Lugano's monthly salary as Louisiana HRS supervisor was $125, raised to $150 early in 1937. Meantime, Lyle Saxon was making $2,900 a year as LWP director. Field supervisors, like Irene Wagner in Baton Rouge, made $100 a month by later 1936, plus a small travel allowance. Some of Lugano's workers received $7 to $10 a month in streetcar tokens, for travel across the Mississippi for work in Gretna, Algiers, and other west bank suburbs of New Orleans.[5]

By streetcar, train, or automobile, HRS workers in New Orleans and Baton Rouge were fanning out into nearby parishes by early 1937. In October, 1936, Lugano had drawn up plans for a so-called second stage of the Louisiana Survey designed to extend the Louisiana HRS beyond the two cities. By October the Louisiana HRS worker quota stood at

4. For Evans' own description of this procedure, see Luther Evans and Edythe Weiner, "The Analysis of County Records," *American Archivist*, I, (October, 1938), 186–200.

5. Luther Evans, "The Local Archives Program of the WPA Historical Records Survey," in Jerome K. Wilcox and A. F. Kuhlman (eds.), *Public Documents with Archives and Libraries* (Chicago: American Library Association, 1938), 284–300; Gaspar Lugano to Luther Evans, December 10, 1936, in Gen. Corr., Louisiana, Box 43, Luther Evans, "Progress Report," June 30, 1936 (typescript in Prof. Rpts., Box 212), both in NA/HRS.

eighty-five. Lugano wanted to assign fifty-one of these to New Orleans and the remaining thirty-four to Baton Rouge. He also wanted
arbitrarily to divide the state into twelve "geographical divisions . . .
suggested only by the convenient operation of the Survey and . . . ir-
respective of any administrative, political, judiciary or electoral jurisdiction of the state." In district one he would list Orleans, Saint
Bernard, Jefferson, Saint Charles, Saint John, Saint James, and Plaquemines parishes. He expected the New Orleans office of the HRS
to continue operations in Orleans Parish but also to move promptly
into the six neighboring parishes in district one. The Baton Rouge office would likewise continue working in East Baton Rouge Parish but
would also move immediately into the other parishes he proposed for
a district four: West Baton Rouge, Pointe Coupee, and East and West
Feliciana. How and when surveys would begin in the ten other divisions that made up the rest of the state he proposed to decide on
later. Then in November, without having implemented his earlier
scheme, he modified it and proposed to divide the state into four sections and to appoint, at salaries of $100 a month, four "traveling field
supervisors" for each section. This scheme, in turn, he (and Saxon)
modified by the end of the year. The New Orleans office by then was
carrying on a modest survey of neighboring parishes, as was the
Baton Rouge office. Two field supervisors had set up headquarters in
Lake Charles to cover neither Lugano's divisions nor his sections but
rather an obvious and existing area, the seventh congressional district. Two more supervisors in Lafayette were to cover congressional
district number five.[6]

By then the HRS had gained separate status from the Federal Writers' Project, and hence Lyle Saxon was no longer available as director
of the Louisiana HRS. Luther Evans had wanted Saxon to remain as
a dual director—of the LWP and the Louisiana HRS. When Saxon
demurred, Evans, not wanting to promote Lugano, offered Edwin
Davis the job as state director of the HRS. Davis agreed to take the
position only if he could serve in a part-time capacity while remain-

6. Lugano to Evans, October 22, November 2, 1936, Saxon to Evans, December 3,
1936, all in Gen. Corr., La., Box 43, NA/HRS; Saxon to Edward Dreyer, November 25,
1936, in 43-11, LHRS.

ing at LSU in Baton Rouge. Evans' superiors in the WPA hierarchy felt Davis to be "thoroughly capable" but preferred a full-time state director and one who would live in New Orleans where the HRS was doing a "greater volume" of work and where the state headquarters of the WPA itself was located. After talking to Saxon in New Orleans, Davis agreed to become state survey advisor (without pay) instead of director, and Saxon agreed to recommend John C. L. Andreassen as state director of the HRS. Andreassen at the time was a twenty-seven-year-old graduate assistant in the LSU history department. With an M.A. from LSU behind him, he was working toward a Ph.D. and trying to support three small children on $50 a month. He had asked Luther Evans for a job in the HRS but got nowhere. He then applied to the New Orleans office of Leo Spofford, state director of the WPA's Woman's and Professional Projects, the agency within which the HRS was then administered. With Davis and Saxon supporting the choice, Spofford hired Andreassen as state director, effective March 10, 1937. Andreassen agreed to retain Lugano as assistant director.[7]

Saxon had been unable to support Lugano for state director. Although Lugano did "good work," he lacked "tact and understanding" in handling workers and in making contacts with local officials in the various parish depositories. Leo Spofford, in the New Orleans WPA office, agreed. Lugano had neither the "personality nor the straight-forwardness necessary." His "broken English" was a handicap, and workers under him suffered from "poor morale." Andreassen, in contrast, had both the personality and the experience needed for the job. During the previous four years, he had plowed through Louisiana constitutions, statutes, and judicial opinions, researching for his M.A. history thesis. Meanwhile, he had worked closely with Davis finding accessions for the LSU Department of Archives, established by the legislature in 1936. According to Davis, Andreassen knew the history

7. Davis to James H. Crutcher (WPA Administrator, Louisiana), December 4, 1936, in 43-11, LHRS; Evans to Saxon, December 9, 1936, in Gen. Corr., La., Box 43, NA/HRS; Crutcher to Evans, October 30, 1936, Evans to Davis, October 16, 1936; Davis to Evans, November 10, 1936, all in Lyle Saxon Papers, Department of Archives, Louisiana State University Library, Baton Rouge; Evans to Saxon, February 2, 1937, in Gen. Corr., La., Box 44, Leo G. Spofford to Blanche M. Ralston (regional director, Women's and Professional Division), February 20, 1937, in Cent. Files, State Ser., La., Box 1435, both in NA/HRS.

of Louisiana "thoroughly" and understood the "purposes and mechanics" of the HRS.[8]

Andreassen was a superb choice as director. At a salary of $2,400 a year, he went on the HRS payroll March 10, 1937, and reported for work in his newly assigned office in the Canal Bank Building in New Orleans. Within days, he had appraised the existing HRS structure and activities and had proposed to Evans some major changes in "procedures and objectives" for the Louisiana Survey, changes that Evans immediately approved. Andreassen wanted his own New Orleans office to assume more—and better—control over all HRS personnel in the state, while at the same time he extended the survey into all parishes. He planned to publish a field manual for "the guidance of survey workers." He outlined a procedure whereby field workers, after they had listed parish records on standardized forms, mailed the inventory to a project supervisor who checked the accuracy and thoroughness of the completed forms. If approved (if not, the forms went back to the field worker), the form then passed to a series of editors in the New Orleans office: receiving clerk, form editor, composing editor, legal editor, and state editor. Having passed through such scrutiny, the parish inventories were typed, assembled in topical or chronological sequence, indexed, and sent to Washington for Evans' approval. Once approved or revised according to Evans' instructions, the inventories were ready for publication.[9]

If Andreassen had an eye for administrative detail, he also appreciated nickels and dimes. Several HRS workers in Baton Rouge who lived across the river in West Baton Rouge Parish asked to be reimbursed for the five-cent ferry ride they took getting to work and back each day. Andreassen suggested they work where they lived, in West Baton Rouge Parish. Whether in accord with this proposal or not, one week later four workers began to survey records in West Baton Rouge Parish. Meantime, while still concentrating on material in New Orleans and Baton Rouge, Andreassen began surveys in several parishes elsewhere—for example, in East Feliciana and Saint John the

8. Saxon to Evans, November 13, 1936, Spofford to Evans, February 18, 1937, both in Gen. Corr., La., Box 43, NA/HRS; John C. L. Andreassen, "Internal Improvements in Louisiana, 1824–1837" (M.A. thesis, Louisiana State University, 1935); Davis to Crutcher, December 4, 1936, in 43-11, LHRS.
9. Andreassen to Evans, March 2, 1937, in 43-11, LHRS.

Baptist on March 29 and in Livingston on April 13. Andreassen himself drove to Pointe Coupee, Avoyelles, and several other parishes for a personal look at records, their storage, and their status. At Houma, in Terrebonne Parish, he found the courthouse "a shambles." The records were "located in a garage" but otherwise were "well kept, carefully bound, and indexed." At Napoleonville in Assumption Parish, he found records housed "in part in a vault, in part in a heap on the wood floors, and in part in a closet dump."[10]

For survey and salvage work in these and other depositories, Andreassen had a quota of seventy-seven workers as of April, 1937; sixty-four (thirteen short of the quota) were then at work. Six of these were "superintendance" class, twenty-five were "professional," thirty-one were "skilled," and two were "intermediate." Of the sixty-four workers, twenty-four were women—with Irene Wagner in Baton Rouge the only female supervisor in the state. Louisiana's quota and its ratio of supervisors to professionals and of men to women was comparable to other state units in Region III of the HRS. For instance, Alabama, with a quota of forty, was employing thirty-four workers, three of them in the superintendance class and thirty of them professional. Evans did find Alabama "overwhelmingly feminized," with only seven males among the thirty-four employees. Mississippi, with a quota of fifty, was employing forty workers, twenty-five of them women. Texas, with the largest quota in the region (120), was using 109 workers, 4 of them in the "superintendance" category, 30 of them professional, 50 of them skilled, and 21 intermediate. Fifty-seven of the workers were women.[11]

After a month on the job Andreassen reported to Evans that inventory of parish records had been completed in eight of the state's sixty-four parishes, though none of these listings had yet reached publication. Besides working in parish inventories, the HRS had also listed records of some 500 churches and seven towns and had done some work in labor and business records and library holdings (at LSU and Tulane). Through the next few months, the Louisiana HRS increased

10. Andreassen to Irene Wagner, March 24, 1937, Andreassen to Edwin A. Davis, March 26, 1937, both in *ibid.*
11. Luther Evans, "Progress Report," April 9, 1937 (typescript in Prg. Rpts., Box 212, NA/HRS).

its quota of workers, extended its range and variety of material surveyed, and began to publish, in mimeographed form, several parish
inventories. Its first publication, the *St. Charles Parish Inventory*, was
an admirable job.[12] Historians praised it, Andreassen was justifiably
proud of it, and Evans held it up as a model for other HRS units in the
nation to follow.

On July 30, Andreassen sent Evans the Saint Charles manuscript,
consisting of 118 entries, on 190 typewritten pages. While waiting for
Evans' response, Andreassen put his typist to work on several completed East Baton Rouge and Terrebonne parish inventories. By this
time Andreassen had arranged with Edwin A. Davis, archivist at
LSU, for the university to publish these and other inventories (that
is, to mimeograph and assemble the typed manuscripts) as soon as
Evans approved them. Although Andreassen was still concentrating
on parish governmental archives as he had declared he would when
he took over the HRS, he was moving workers into other areas as
well. The Baton Rouge office was listing city as well as parish records.
Under Irene Wagner's supervision, workers had drawn up a reliable
and comprehensive list of churches, by the simple expedient of going
to the files of the clerk of court and examining his listing of tax-
exempt property. In this way, they identified ninety-nine churches by
name, location, denomination, and race. By midsummer of 1937, at
the Louisiana State Museum in New Orleans, about one hundred
WPA workers, not all of them HRS personnel, were at work translating, briefing, indexing, and binding material there. From this work,
several publications would emerge in the period, 1937–1942. Meanwhile, as he was administering all this activity, Andreassen lost one
competent assistant but promptly added another one. In June, Irene
Wagner resigned from the HRS because of poor health. She regretted
the necessity, for she liked her job. She told Andreassen that, as a
"real life situation from which to obtain an education in history and
local government," her job had been "superior to any college course
in these fields of study." Vergil Bedsole replaced Wagner in Baton

12. *Ibid.*; *St. Charles Parish Inventory* (Baton Rouge: Department of Archives, Louisiana State University, 1937), Vol. XLV of *Inventory of the Parish Archives of Louisiana*. Each
parish inventory was numbered according to its position in the alphabetical list of the
parishes; hence the volume number attached to the first parish inventory to appear.

Rouge as project supervisor; soon he would become assistant supervisor in New Orleans, along with Lugano who held the same title.[13]

Luther Evans found the indexing and editing under the Andreassen administration "highly satisfactory." The total cost of the HRS project for the fiscal year July 1, 1936–June 30, 1937, was $61,165, which covered 824 "man-months" of employment at an average man-month cost of $74.20. Louisiana compared favorably to most other states in Region III in what the HRS produced for the money it spent. Alabama, for instance, had cost much less ($22,511 for the fiscal year), but Evans judged that the state needed "a more aggressive director and a first class editor." Editorial work in Arkansas was "distinctly below average." In Region III, only North Carolina was a match for Louisiana in quality of output. The North Carolina HRS, which was turning out "eminently satisfactory" work at a total cost of $65,849 for the 1936–37 fiscal year, had impressed Evans from the beginning. Outside Region III, state HRS units ranged from the indifferent to the meticulous. Costs in New Mexico for the fiscal year totaled $31,774. The project, with about forty workers, was "not well administered," and editorial instructions from Washington were "treated with indifference." On the other hand, Maine, with about forty workers and at a cost of $40,186, was "very satisfactory" and was doing "unusually meticulous" editing. The Louisiana HRS, though never subject to adverse criticism from Evans, under Andreassen's direction gradually improved in quality until, by November, 1937, Evans approved a regional supervisor's report that the Louisiana HRS was "undoubtedly the best in the South."[14] The Saint Charles Parish inventory, submitted to Evans on July 30, had pleased him, though he found many things for Andreassen to do to it before publication.

On September 1, 1937, Evans returned the Saint Charles inventory to Andreassen. To Evans it "represent[ed] a great deal of careful and painstaking work"—in some cases too much work. Introductory essays that Andreassen, Lugano, and others had compiled came to five

13. Andreassen, "Semi-Monthly Progress Report," May, June, July, 1937 (typescripts in 43-11, LHRS). Wagner to Andreassen, June 18, 1937, in Gen. Corr., La., Box 44, NA/HRS.

14. Evans, "Progress Report," October 13, 1937 (typescript in Prg. Rpts., Box 212), Evans memo, November 6, 1937, in Cent. Files, State Ser., La., Box 1435, both in NA/HRS.

times the number of pages devoted to the entries themselves, and Evans thought this proportion "not desirable." On the other hand, he wanted more information on some things. Andreassen had attached to the inventory a little essay on the history of Saint Charles Parish. Evans thought it was "very good" but wanted Andreassen to add material on the languages once or currently spoken there and data on agriculture and industry in the parish to provide a "better picture of the present life and conditions of the parish." The charts of governmental organization that Andreassen had included needed to be clarified. Evans sent Andreassen a copy of a chart done by the Missouri HRS and suggested that he follow it, with due modification for Louisiana's differences. Evans also called for numerous minor changes in format and usage: do not abbreviate "courthouse"; combine several essays on several parish courts into one and condense the resulting synthesis; recheck cross-references, some of which were in error; let the table of contents show all subject headings included in the inventory proper.[15]

Evans' detailed critique and intensive editing arose from pleasure with the work, not pique. Once Andreassen had revised the Saint Charles volume following Evans' suggestions, prepared an index, and returned the manuscript to Washington for approval, Evans was confident that the inventory would be ready for publication. Andreassen and his New Orleans staff went to work on the manuscript. HRS workers had done their original survey of the parish archives between November 16 and December 7, 1936. They returned for a recheck on April 30, and finished on May 21, 1937. For the "completeness and accuracy" of the inventory, Andreassen held the parish workers responsible. His office staff in New Orleans, under his direction, had contributed the introductory essays and edited the manuscript that had gone to Evans in July. In the six weeks after Evans returned it for further editing, the New Orleans staff made the necessary revisions, received approval from Evans to publish it, and in mid-December began a strategic distribution of copies to selected people in Louisiana and Washington. The LSU Archives, which had published the inventory in mimeographed form, hoped to raise sup-

15. Evans to Andreassen, September 1, 1937, in 43-11, LHRS.

port—and money—for more publications. The clerk of court in each parish received a copy, along with a letter from Andreassen asking if the clerk or other officials wanted more such volumes done. Copies went to the White House, to Harry Hopkins at the WPA, to Louisiana Senator Allen J. Ellender, and to several lawyers and educators in Louisiana.[16]

Virtually everyone who acknowledged receipt of the inventory offered a polite, if banal, comment on it and asked for more volumes in the series. One historian at Natchitoches liked it but found "slight errors that would seriously hinder its maximum effectiveness." He promised to send Andreassen a list of "corrections." In New Orleans the state director of the WPA Woman's and Professional Projects liked the inventory but regretted that it was mimeographed rather than printed. The *Journal of Southern History*, then being published at LSU and edited by Wendell H. Stephenson of the LSU history department, took special note of the inventory. The *Journal* listed several new HRS inventories recently published in Texas, North Carolina, and elsewhere, and then singled out the Saint Charles volume for comment. The inventory represented "research, compilation, and editing at their best." As useful as the inventory itself were several items in the introduction: the essay on "Housing, Care, and Accessibility of the Records," charts showing government organization at several different periods, an essay on "the evolution of . . . parish government," and a "brief but authoritative sketch of the parish." The historical sketch contained "literally thousands of citations to constitutions, codes, acts, and revised statutes, and to the most authoritative secondary sources." A "careful check" by the *Journal* revealed that research for the essay had been "accurate, exhaustive, and meticulous."[17]

If the *St. Charles Inventory* became a model for subsequent parish inventories in Louisiana and county inventories in other states, it was partly because of the skill and scholarship that Andreassen and his staff had brought to their task. But the larger concept of the county-

16. *Ibid.*; John Andreassen, "Preface," in *St. Charles Inventory*; "J. Andreassen, 1937" folder, in 43-11, "Andreassen Corr., 1938" folder, in 43-12, both in LHRS.

17. John Kyser to Andreassen, January 5, 1938, in "Andreassen Corr., 1938" folder, 43-12, LHRS. Leo G. Spofford to Davis, December 17, 1937, in 43-11, LHRS; "Historical News and Notices," *The Journal of Southern History*, IV (February, 1938), 127–28.

parish inventory—the form and structure, the categories and headings—came from Evans himself. He imposed his own design upon the HRS surveys, focused attention on county records, and demanded introductory essays on the history and political structure of the county, which these records reflected. Questions of just what a *record* was, how it should be listed and described, whether it should be listed under more than one heading, and whether the HRS should impose some given order or rearrangement upon the material that workers so often found in utter disarray bothered Evans and forced him to formulate some principles for workers to follow in analyzing and listing county records. And Evans always insisted that in the HRS program it was local records—county and town—that had priority.[18]

The Saint Charles Parish inventory, distinctive though it was, was only one among some 200 inventories published or approved for publication by all HRS units up to June, 1939. And in style and substance they all showed the editorial impact of Luther Evans. By June 1, inventories had been completed in 1,809 of the nation's 3,066 counties, and in 1,459 cities and towns. The county inventories averaged 130 mimeographed pages per volume. Of each 100 pages, 3 contained historical sketches, 2 or 3 offered essays on housing and care of records, and 31 presented essays on government organization and records systems and the powers and duties of county office. The historical sketches were the nearest thing to history that HRS personnel ever wrote. This was comparable to the work of the Federal Writers' Project, which hired few writers and produced little that would fall in the realm of imaginative literature (though the major output of the FWP, the guidebooks, were brilliant works of their genre). The HRS hired few historians, except for supervisory personnel such as Andreassen in Louisiana, most HRS workers did strictly clerical chores, and most HRS publications were listings, inventories, and guides designed to lead historians, lawyers, and other professionals to the sources, from which they might themselves learn or write history. Evans thought the county histories included in each county inventory were a "considerable contribution" to the history of counties in America; each such history was written in "some degree" from the

18. Evans and Weiner, "The Analysis of County Records."

sources that HRS workers found in doing the very inventory of the county. Still, these county histories were modest in size and overwhelmingly political in perspective, as were the remaining introductory essays. Evans wanted the essays on governmental organization to give "a complete and precise account of all constitutional and statutory provisions concerning county agencies of government and their records." He believed that the work by the HRS would "lay the basis for a definitive study of the development and present status of county government in the United States." But HRS personnel could hardly do this study by themselves. In mid-1938, the HRS was carrying about 3,000 workers on its rolls. Ninety-five percent of them had been certified for relief and had neither the training nor the incentive to write history. Even so, Evans was pleased that they had shown "a special aptitude for accepting training in the type of work being [done] by the Survey." Evans could only "rejoice" that the HRS had produced "technical work of good quality" and at the same time had "fulfilled the basic responsibility of WPA to keep workers busy at tasks which will prevent the deterioration of their morale and their skill." [19]

This was the perspective on the HRS that Evans held in mid-1937, and activity in Louisiana the rest of the year under Andreassen's direction did little to change and much to confirm that perspective. By September 30, Andreassen had his full quota of personnel—sixty—at work in fourteen parishes. They had surveyed and revised seven parish inventories and had edited six more that were now ready for typing and mimeographing. None would be published until the end of the year, when the Saint Charles Inventory appeared. In mid-November Evans raised the Louisiana quota to sixty-five, after receiving a field supervisor's report that the Louisiana HRS was the "best in the South and that additional workers are badly needed." But the sixty-five workers were barely visible in most parishes. On December 1, thirty-one men and thirty-four women were at work in eighteen parishes. Twenty-eight were in Orleans parish, and fifteen were in East Baton Rouge. In the other sixteen parishes, sometimes two but usually one solitary worker was burrowing into the parish archives,

19. Evans, "The Local Archives Program of the WPA," 284–300.

ranging in energy from inertia to diligence. By December 31, Andreassen reported that his staff had "entered" thirty-one parishes. In sixteen of the parishes they had completed inventories, and the drafts of
nine other inventories were ready for editing. Meantime, Andreassen
was acquiring support for forthcoming publications. The Louisiana
Historical Association had agreed to publish manuscript calendars
during the coming six months, "whatever the cost." The Department
of Middle American Research at Tulane would publish whatever inventories the HRS made of that department's archives.[20]

In December, when Andreassen began to circulate the *St. Charles
Inventory*, ten other states also issued their first publication, like Louisiana, in mimeographed form. Evans had asked each state HRS to
publish an inventory by the end of the year. Although it barely made
that deadline, the *St. Charles Inventory* gave the Louisiana HRS a good
name compared to reports Evans was receiving for two-thirds or more
of the states. Appraising the states that had not yet published inventories by January 1, 1938, Evans again and again cited incompetent
state directors as the primary culprits. In Arkansas work was "distinctly unsatisfactory," and Evans feared that "acceptable work cannot be done under the present project director." Arizona was "another case of an incompetent director." Delaware's failure to publish
was due to "administrative incompetence" and an emphasis on church
records at the expense of county archives. Maine's delay in publishing arose not from incompetent direction but from excessive rechecking and revision of inventories "in an effort to gain perfection." Evans, after being "kidded along" by Montana for many months with
the claim that workers were doing good field work but that good editors were hard to find, had "gotten tough" on the state director, a university professor on part-time duty with the HRS who had been "letting us down." Evans thought Montana would "illustrate how active
such a man can become when the griddle gets hot." Nebraska, "one
of the most unsatisfactory of all [HRS] projects," had a director "who

20. Andreassen, "Semi-Monthly Report," September 30, 1937, December 15, 1937
(typescripts in "Andreassen, 1937" file, 43-11, LHRS). The sixteen were Allen, Beau-
regard, East Feliciana, Livingston, Natchitoches, Pointe Coupee, Red River, Sabine,
Saint Helena, Saint Tammany, and West Feliciana with one worker each; and Avoyelles,
Calcasieu, Jefferson Davis, Rapides, and Tangipahoa with two workers each. "Semi-
Monthly Reports," November 16, 1937.

lacks initiative and who procrastinates beyond all reason." Nebraska would "improve rapidly or we will have a new director." In New Jersey the problem seemed to be both money and supervisors—the latter wanting more of the former before turning out any work. Evans thought the New Jersey supervisors "unduly persistent in demanding salary increases" and determined that they were demanding "more credit and . . . more cash than they deserve or will receive." Such an attitude was "of course not enjoyed exclusively by the New Jersey Project." [21]

Neither Andreassen nor the Louisiana HRS expressed New Jersey's undue self-esteem or its plea for more money. Andreassen and his supervisory staff had, by the beginning of 1938, begun to receive credit for the quality of their work. Andreassen, at a salary of $200 a month, was receiving a bit more than the national average of $180 for full-time directors. And Evans continued to raise Louisiana's quota, even while Andreassen contined to "enter" more parishes and to ready more inventories for publication. [22] In 1938 a larger and larger quota of workers would sustain the quality and dramatically increase the quantity of surveys that Louisiana made and published. And Andreassen himself would assume supervision of HRS activity well beyond Louisiana.

21. Evans, "Progress Report," December 16–31, 1937, in Prg. Rpts., Box 212, NA/HRS.

22. *Ibid.*; Memorandum, in "Andreassen, 1937" folder, 43-11, LHRS.

IV. *State and Local Americana*

Early in 1938, Evans began to consider appointing Andreassen an HRS field supervisor. In addition to directing the Louisiana survey, Andreassen would make periodic inspection trips to neighboring state units, as well. It was a good idea. By March, after one year as state director, Andreassen had become a skillful and diligent administrator. He had taken charge in Louisiana and was steadily expanding HRS work in the state. He obviously had the ability to continue his work in Louisiana and at the same time inspect and evaluate other state HRS offices and advise them on ways to bring their work up to the Louisiana level. In February he drew up an instruction manual for workers to use in doing surveys of municipal archives. Defining *towns* as communities of 1,000 to 1,500 people, and *cities* as incorporated areas of 5,000 or more inhabitants, he counted 105 cities and towns in Louisiana. Work had barely begun in these archives; he reported a "first listing" accomplished in eighteen municipalities and only one "first draft inventory" (for New Orleans) prepared and ready to send to Washington for approval. But as his new manual indicated, he intended the municipal surveys to be as thorough as were the parish inventories and to contain the same kind of historical and political introductions that he and Evans had designed for the county-parish inventories.[1] Meantime, a few HRS workers—Gaspar Lugano among

1. Luther Evans to Ellen Woodward, February 27, 1938, in Central Files, State Series, Box H-M, Woodward to James H. Crutcher, March 1, 1939, in General Correspondence, Louisiana, Box 45, both in Record Group No. 69 (Work Projects Administration), National Archives, hereinafter cited as NA/HRS; John Andreassen, "Monthly State Progress Report," January, 1938 (typescript in 43-11), Andreassen, "Manual: Municipal Ar-

them—had continued to inventory church records, primarily in New Orleans. Andreassen had found Lugano "unable to handle editorial work on parish inventories" and had placed him in charge of the church inventories. When he discovered that an editor working under Lugano's supervision was faking record entries, Andreassen fired the editor. Then when Andreassen personally checked some entries that Lugano himself had made and found numerous errors, he put Lugano onto translations of French and Spanish documents in New Orleans archives. In this work, Lugano was "extremely competent." Even so, if Lugano did not "work out" here, Andreassen would "be ready to release him." By April, in light of the work underway by the Louisiana HRS and Andreassen's role in administering it, Evans found the Louisiana unit to be "outstanding," though "not before Mr. Andreassen's appointment a year ago." [2]

In March Evans decided to send Andreassen into several southern states to inspect HRS work then underway and to assist in final editing of these states' inventories. In March, Andreassen made his first inspection trip as acting field supervisor to Alabama and Mississippi. In April he made an extended trip, visiting HRS offices in Arkansas, Florida, Mississippi, and Georgia in Region III, and about seven offices in the Midwest. He sent Evans recommendations on quotas and evaluations of the work of each unit he visited. In April, Evans raised his annual salary to $2,900. By then, in view of his efficiency, Andreassen was earning every dollar he drew, but some of his staff were not so productive. In May, while he was out of the state on a field trip, two workers in New Orleans—one of them a former city editor on the New Orleans *Item* who was, in Andreassen's opinion, "our most promising writer"— showed up for work drunk and were promptly fired. When Andreassen returned to New Orleans, he found that one of his editors, named Hunt, was hospitalized with a heart ailment. Before Hunt left the job for the hospital and perhaps to

chives Inventory," (printed copy) both in HRS Papers, Department of Archives, Louisiana State University Library, Baton Rouge, hereinafter cited as LHRS.

2. Andreassen to Evans, March 4, 1938, in Gen. Corr., La., Box 45, Evans, "Progress Report," April 1, 1938 (typescript in Box 212), Evans to Harry Hopkins, April 1, 1938, in Cent. Files, Stat Ser., La., Box H-M, all in NA/HRS.

explain his heart condition, he wrote a memorandum about his own problems with HRS forms as well as the problems being suffered by entry editor Louis Hermann:

We have judgments, releases and acts of correction,
Petitions, citations and proofs of succession,
With transfers, indentures and mineral assignments,
Exchanges, adoptions and judicial confinements,
Last testaments, wills and acts of donation,
Partial releases and tax-subrogation,
Tutorships, patents, bonds and restrictions,
Redemptions, agreements, writs and convictions,
Crop liens, partitions, inquests, revisions,
Pleadings and true-bills and judges' decisions.
To you my dear friend, this may seem a bit hazy,
But this is the reason why Hermann is crazy.

If Hermann was crazy, perhaps it was because of the editing he had to do on the listings he sometimes received from workers in the parishes. When H. F. Faust, a worker in Natchitoches, despaired over trying to decipher the "torn and faded" records he was listing, he decided to "trace" what he turned in to New Orleans. As he explained, "the words being confusing, I thought perhaps it was best to trace direct from the record." If this was agreeable to the New Orleans editors, Faust would do more of it, but in that case he had a request: "please forward me some transparent paper."[3]

Faust was conscientious and even imaginative, not inept and lazy. The documents he was listing—Original Instruments, Records of Conveyances, August 1, 1738, to May 31, 1765—were, indeed, ragged and dirty and hard to decipher. Faust in Natchitoches was discovering what HRS workers all over the country were also learning: county archives were a mess. In March, 1938, when he testified before a U.S. Senate committee then considering a bill to create a Bureau of Fine Arts, Evans made a cogent and forceful case for the rescue work being done by the HRS. The "basic purpose" of the Survey, he informed the committee, was to prepare inventories and other bibliographical guides that would "render more accessible the great masses of un-

3. "Andreassen Correspondence, 1938," in 43-11, LHRS; Woodward to Crutcher, April 11, 1938, Andreassen to Evans, June 2, 3, 1938, all in Gen. Corr., La., 1938, NA/HRS.

published official documents" in state and local depositories throughout the country. These bibliographies could serve as handbooks for officials who, in doing their jobs, needed to examine the records left by their predecessors. The guides would also be useful to those numerous other citizens in the land who made up a very "army of researchers interested in . . . American civilization." Essential data on government, law, military affairs, bridges, sewers, religion, art, and other subjects were available in the public records of the nation—if the HRS could only uncover and salvage material from the cesspools and rotting storehouses into which most of the records had been shoved. In 1938 there were 3,066 counties (including the Louisiana parishes) and "uncounted thousands" of towns, cities, and other local units of government in the United States. Their records, like those of many libraries and historical societies, were sometimes well preserved and easily accessible. But the vast majority were unorganized and unlabeled "mountainous heaps," containing thousands of tons of unsorted and unknown documents, some of them priceless, some of them rubbish.[4]

Evans did not amplify his claim in any detail, though he later received from Tennessee a graphic testimonial to the trashy dumps that many archives had become. In one Tennessee county, records had been "literally dumped and piled for years, some on shelves and many on the floor." HRS workers had to "shovel out dead rats, disinfect the room, and hook up a suction fan" before they could begin to organize and index the records. In another county, records in a basement hallway were mixed with rats, spiders, roaches, flies, and fleas. The rats were in "various stages of decomposition." The records were "utterly without order." Two strong young National Youth Administration workers used a wheelbarrow, a shovel, an axe, and two gallons of insecticide to clean the room, then whitewashed the walls and painted the woodwork, and the HRS workers arranged, labeled, and catalogued the records. They then discovered another storage room even richer in animate and inanimate matter. Besides the ubiquitous

---

4. Luther Evans, "The Historical Records Survey: A Statement on Its Program and Accomplishments Presented to the Sub-Committee of the Senate Committee on Education and Labor, in Connection with the Bill to Create a Permanent Bureau of Fine Arts, March 1, 1938" (mimeograph copy in "HRS circular" file, 43-12, LHRS).

rats, there were roaches, flies, fleas, mosquitoes, corn, oats, bridles, paint, tin cans, corncobs, skulls, and "swords and robes of a defunct secret order." Out of this stinking mess, the HRS found and labeled and bound some 200 volumes, 650 bundles, and 150 file boxes of circuit court records. Since then the room, "formerly almost never entered," was used every day by attorneys and public officials.[5]

If Evans deplored the filth and chaos that the HRS found in its salvage work and the disinterest and ignorance about the past that this implied, he was rhapsodic over what these salvage operations meant to American culture. The work of the HRS was "part of a great movement which is sweeping America along to a historical renaissance." Americans were taking more and more pride in their accomplishments and were achieving "more dignity and richness" as they studied their past "in the only way that it can be studied," namely, in the source materials that the HRS was making "adequately accessible to us for the first time."[6]

Evans was, of course, making a case for his own agency before a Senate committee that might give it permanent status within a proposed Bureau of Fine Arts, though Evans opposed that idea. By 1938 several bills had been introduced into Congress to make parts or all of the emergency Four Arts program permanent agencies and functions of government.[7] Not for another generation, with establishment of the National Foundation on the Arts and the Humanities in 1965, would any such federal patronage become available, but Evans, in his 1938 testimony to the Senate committee, was expressing an attitude toward American history and culture that had already developed during the Depression decade. As Warren Susman, for one, has so forcefully demonstrated, it was in the 1930s that Americans, who had always been much preoccupied with their "mission" in the world and with their very purpose and identity on the American continent,

---

5. T. Marshall Jones (state director, Tennessee HRS) to Evans, memo, October 12, 1938 (copy in *ibid.*)

6. Evans, "The HRS: A Statement."

7. The most notable of these were the Coffee-Pepper bill (by Congressman John M. Coffee of Washington and Senator Claude Pepper of Florida) to create a Bureau of Fine Arts, and various proposals by Congressman William I. Sorovich of New York to add a department of science, art, and literature to the cabinet. Richard D. McKinzie, *The New Deal for Artists* (Princeton: Princeton University Press, 1973), 151ff., discusses the fate of these proposals.

came to full belief that there was such a thing as an "American way of life." In the decade of the thirties, more than ever before, they set out to discover, define, and portray that way of life in all its rich eclecticism and contradictions, to photograph it, to record it, to inventory it, and to save it, first from the threat of economic collapse within, then from the threat of fascism abroad.[8] The HRS, with its urge to recover the detailed public records of American life, was one tangible manifestation of this cultural nationalism that so characterized the 1930s. Meantime, however much they identified with an "American way of life" or pondered its fate and the usefulness and meaning of the records they were salvaging, to hundreds of HRS workers the Survey meant something more prosaic and fundamental: it meant a job in a time of desperate need.

Evans himself realized that it was the crisis of the Depression that had brought the HRS into being and that had enabled him to put 2,800 workers on the HRS payroll by mid-1938. Evans took pride in the Survey, and he told Harry Hopkins that the HRS was rapidly becoming "an accepted institution of government, with a very definite role to play in local and national affairs, rather than a fly-by-night concern engaged in work of dubious validity and doubtful value." Yet Evans opposed inclusion of the Survey in the proposed Bureau of Fine Arts. The HRS belonged just where it was—in the WPA, created to provide work relief in the emergency of the Great Depression. Congress would simply not appropriate to an independent or a permanent Survey "anything like the quarter of a million dollars per month" that Evans was spending by April, 1938. As it was, Evans wanted a thousand more workers for the HRS.[9]

Evans' judgment of the HRS is hardly surprising. He had conceived the Survey, had seen it gradually take form, gain momentum, and prove its worth; what it needed now was not institutional permanence but a little more time and money to finish the task it was then

---

8. Warren Susman (ed.), *Culture and Commitment, 1929–1945* (New York: George Braziller, 1973). The literature on this theme is rich. It begins, perhaps, with Alfred Kazin's brilliant chapter, "America! America!" in *On Native Grounds* (New York: Harcourt, Brace, 1942), and has received close inspection and analysis recently in such studies as William Stott, *Documentary Expression and Thirties America* (New York: Oxford University Press, 1973).

9. Evans to Hopkins, April 1, 1938, in Prg. Rpts., Box 212, NA/HRS.

doing—and doing well. Whether his claims were self-serving or not, whether he was right about most state surveys or not, Louisiana in 1938 exemplified Evans' testimony to HRS efficiency. Some state surveys, though already doing good work, had improved enough to gain "special mention" in Evans' April report to WPA headquarters. In three other states—Louisiana, Ohio, and Pennsylvania—"refinements of inventory work" had increased to such a degree that they were "among the leading projects" in the nation.[10]

Perhaps for this reason, Evans raised the Louisiana quota sharply, and by late summer, 1938, the Louisiana HRS was carrying about 330 workers on its payroll. As always, the distribution was lopsided: nearly 200 workers were on the job in New Orleans, and the remainder were scattered around the state, with at least one (and usually just one) worker in thirty-nine of the state's fifty-nine parishes. Fifty-six of the two hundred workers in New Orleans were making entries for the Early American Imprints program, an ambitious (but ultimately aborted) scheme to list all early books, pamphlets, and broadsides printed in each state before 1876 (or before 1890 in eight Western states, where printing began later than in the East). As New Orleans supervisor Vergil Bedsole pointed out, this emphasis on imprints in the Crescent City was due to the concentration of libraries there, ranging from the New Orleans public library to the university libraries at Tulane, Loyola, Xavier, and Dillard, as well as those at the Louisiana State Museum and several small colleges and institutes in the city. Even so, the state university in Baton Rouge merited more than the one worker doing imprints there, as did Louisiana Normal in Natchitoches, which had been assigned two imprint workers. The work on the imprints increased through the fall, with sixty-eight workers carried on the roll in November. By then, most of the work had been done and by January, 1939, only thirty-six workers were still assigned to Imprints. In his supervisor's report at year's end, Bedsole reported that during 1938 the Survey had checked 1,077 different "institutions" in Orleans parish for their holdings of American imprints. This had included "associations, lodges, asylums, churches, medical clinics, convents, hospitals, museums, newspapers, printers, and publish-

10. Evans to Ellen Woodward, May 4, 1938, in Cent. Files, State Ser., Box H-M, NA/ HRS.

ers," as well as the more obvious university and library holdings. By December 31, 1938, workers in New Orleans and elsewhere in the state had typed over 12,000 entries, and Andreassen's office had edited them and sent them to the imprints headquarters in Chicago.[11]

Work in municipal archives of the parish was more nearly equitable between New Orleans and the rest of the state than was the imprint program. During 1938 the Department of Archives at LSU published five of the parish inventories in the series of fifty-nine that Andreassen had projected: *Lafayette Parish* (Lafayette) in February; *Calcasieu Parish* (Lake Charles) in March; *Allen Parish* (Oberlin) in June; *Natchitoches Parish* (Natchitoches) in September; and *St. Bernard Parish* (Saint Bernard) in December. The remainder of the Survey's staff, during the year, inventoried church archives and labor union records, indexed court records and acts of the state legislature, transcribed police jury minutes, and translated and catalogued manuscript collections.

Out of all this browsing and digging and recording would come several dozen publications in the next three years, but the most notable output, apart from the parish inventories, would be the police jury transcriptions. Initial work on these minutes began in Baton Rouge in April, 1938, when two workers began thumbing through the earliest extant volume of the East Baton Rouge Parish police jury minutes, for the year 1847. By August, 1938, field workers were doing a word for word, page for page transcription of police jury minutes in twenty-two parishes. At least one volume had been transcribed (but not yet published) in every parish by the end of 1938. As usual, the New Orleans area—in this case Jefferson Parish—received earliest and greatest attention, with thirteen volumes transcribed in 5,056 pages.[12] The Jefferson Parish minutes were the first to gain publication, two volumes appearing early in 1939; eventually, twenty-four

11. Douglas C. McMurtrie, "A Nationwide Inventory of American Imprints Under WPA Auspices," in Jerome K. Wilcox and A. F. Kuhlman (eds.), *Public Documents with Archives and Libraries* (Chicago: American Library Association, 1938), 301–316; Bedsole to Evans, August 19, 1938, Bedsole to Alma Hammond, March 3, 1939, both in Gen. Corr., La., Box 45, NA/HRS; William C. Bennett, "Catalogs and Finding Lists of Louisiana Source Materials" (copy of a paper read by Bennett, supervisor, La. Imprints Inventory, before Louisiana Library Association Meeting, Lafayette, April 16, 1940, in 43-12, LHRS).
12. Bedsole to Hammond, March 3, 1939, in 43-11, LHRS.

volumes drawn from Iberville, Jefferson, and Saint Bernard parishes appeared in print.

Either because they felt the appreciation for American artifacts and local color that social historians attribute to the 1930s or simply because they were trying to cover the state and find everything subject to being listed or indexed or transcribed, the Louisiana HRS poked into an incredible range of basements, garrets, cribs, boxes, and agencies both public and private. Workers in New Orleans peered into records of the Boiler and Smoke Division of the Department of Safety, the parish prison, and the parish teachers' retirement fund. In Baton Rouge, they worked in the Department of Archives and Manuscripts at LSU, where in March the HRS unloaded twelve truckloads of state archival material rescued from the old state capitol. One task force examined every act passed by the legislature from 1804 to 1938 and copied those considered "useful" to Andreassen's essayists and forms editors. Gaspar Lugano, assigned to translate documents from French and Spanish into English, proved Andreassen's judgment on him—that in this field he was "extremely competent"—and at the same time justified Evans' decision to allow the Louisiana HRS to do translations, one of the very few states granted such a program. Lugano and his staff ranged over south Louisiana, digging through manuscripts at LSU, at Howard Memorial Library in New Orleans, and in archives of territorial courts in New Orleans.[13]

Perhaps it was this attention to the job at hand, this conscientious attempt to carry out the program that Evans had envisioned and that Andreassen had moved into with such alacrity, that led Evans in August, 1938, to ask Andreassen to join his staff in Washington, as deputy national director, at a salary of $3,600. Andreassen chose, for the time being, to remain in Louisiana while continuing to serve as acting field supervisor with headquarters in New Orleans. Already, since March, he had made a number of "trouble shooting" trips, as Evans called them. In December, Evans asked him to go to Tallahassee to see how the Florida office was being run. "I can't tell," said Evans, "whether they know what they are doing." Andreassen's inspection

13. *Ibid*; Andreassen to Evans, March 4, 1938, in Gen. Corr., La., Box 45, NA/HRS; Evans, "Progress Report," April 1, 1938.

tours did not lessen his supervision over Louisiana personnel. He continued to file reports with Evans detailing the work going on in the state, the caliber of the personnel, and the checking and rechecking he demanded of them. And in March, 1939, as he had done several times before, he proposed some changes in the county inventories that by now were coming in to Evans from surveys all over the nation. Each of these inventories, as the Evans format demanded, contained a historical sketch of the county. These were often superficial, hurriedly written, and all but bereft of reliable documentation. Andreassen described a method (evidently the kind he had worked out for Louisiana) whereby the professional, or at least experienced, supervisors or editors in a state's home office would use the HRS clerical force around the state to do the basic research in what these clerks knew best: namely, the files they were currently indexing. To obtain material from a local newspaper, supervisors needed only to examine the index already done on the paper, and from this select a story or item in the paper, and let the local worker copy the material. The same could be done with workers indexing manuscripts, church archives, imprints, and all the other sources the HRS was uncovering. All the material the HRS discovered and listed could be used as a source for the historical sketch done for each county. "Anyone who can read and write," said Andreassen, "can get the material into a state office where better talent can be used [to write the sketch]." To Andreassen, this was not the ideal way to produce good history. But the HRS lacked the trained personnel, the time, and the money to produce "comprehensive local studies" of each county. The next best thing was a scheme such as his that would at least produce sketches explaining "how there came to be a county and the records we inventory." William R. Hogan, assistant archivist at LSU (he would receive a Ph.D. at the University of Texas in 1942), thought the historical essays were "usually not equal in quality to the inventories to which they serve as introduction." And, too, they contained too many "divergencies into such matters as religion, education, the press, industry, agriculture, social background of settlers, emigration, transportation, mail routes, mineral resources, tavern prices, apprentice contracts, military movements, ghost towns, tornadoes, a record flood, and other acts of God." [14] At best, this kind of detail portrayed the society that had developed in the county; at worst it was a grab bag of anecdotes, presented without order, coherence, or meaning.

Evans had hoped for the best but often received the worst kind. He periodically tried to improve the historical sketches. From the inception of the HRS, he had insisted that it focus most of its attention on local and county records, and also from the beginning had demanded that historical sketches accompany each county inventory. Shortly after receiving Andreassen's suggestions, Evans wrote a stinging fifteen-page critique of an unsatisfactory inventory he had received from Ohio. He mimeographed this and sent it as a memorandum to all state HRS directors with the remark that "these comments should be considered when compiling inventories from your state." [15]

The good county histories that Evans and Andreassen wanted and sometimes got may be viewed as the HRS counterpart to the more celebrated guidebooks done for each state by the FWP. In turn, the HRS county studies and the FWP state studies can be cited as further evidence of the cultural nationalism—or better still, a kind of cultural regionalism—that coursed through American culture and scholarship in the 1930s. Except among genealogists, antiquarians, and largely "amateur" historians, state and local history had never flourished in the United States. From their appearance about 1885, professional historians in the United States had written more about presidents and Congress than about mayors and city councils. Robert Binkley said it well in the mid-1930s: Americans had long been one of the most backward peoples in the world in the organization of localized information. At about the same time that Luther Evans was picking up ideas from Binkley and other historians and was planning the HRS with its focus on the American county, the new FWP directors were drawing on ideas from poets and novelists and literary critics and gradually formulating the scheme to produce state guidebooks.

14. Evans memo, August 8, 1939, Evans to Andreassen, December 13, 1938, Andreassen to Evans, March 13, 1939, all in Gen. Corr., La., Box 45, NA/HRS; William R. Hogan, "The Historical Records Survey: An Outside View" (copy of a paper read on October 13, 1939, at annual meeting of Society of American Archivists, Annapolis, Md., in 43-11, LHRS).

15. Evans to Andreassen, May 5, 1939, memo, in "Papers by HRS Personnel" folder, 43-12, LHRS.

Like that for the county inventories and the introductory essays that accompanied them, the basic data that went into the state guides was dug out of old books and newspapers and archives—and from tombstones and churches and chamber of commerce handouts. Like Andreassen's editors using data sent in from the field by clerks, the Writers' Project editors would actually write the guidebooks. Some of these contained brilliant sketches, such as poet Conrad Aiken's essay on Deerfield, Massachusetts, in that state's guidebook. Some, as an otherwise admiring critic wrote in 1938, were "stuffy" (Maine), or "tiresomely sententious" (Mississippi). In several states the WPA director himself did much of the research and wrote most if not all of the guidebook, as did Vardis Fisher in Idaho. In Louisiana Lyle Saxon and his assistant Robert Tallant were responsible for the high quality of the state guide.[16]

Whatever their quality and however produced, all the guidebooks had one element in common, which they shared with the HRS county inventories: their compilers had discovered the United States, all forty-eight of them, and the localities and peculiar characters within each one. As a perceptive reader, novelist Robert Cantwell, observed in 1939, "None of the generalizations about Americans seems to fit the people described in the Guides—creepy and cranky Americans, others with a lunatic sense of humor for names and tombstone jingles, others who decide ownership of property by flipping a coin, still others who built spite fences and spite churches, in places like Backus Corner, Maine, or Baboon Gulch, Idaho, or Cantwell's Bridge, Delaware." Of course, as a member of the FWP staff judged the guides later, much of this portraiture was "fantasy," and the FWP writers engaged in "mindless trivialities" under the delusion that they were en-

16. Robert C. Binkley, "The Cultural Program of the W.P.A.," *Harvard Educational Review*, IX (March, 1939), 156–74; Kathleen McKinzie, "Writers on Relief" (Ph.D. dissertation, Indiana University, 1970); Katharine Kellock, "The WPA Writers: Portraitists of the United States," *American Scholar*, IX (1940), 473–82; Monty Noam Penkower, *The Federal Writers' Project: A Study in Government Patronage of the Arts* (Urbana: University of Illinois Press, 1977), 21ff; Ray Allen Billington, "Government and the Arts: The W.P.A. Experience," *American Quarterly*, XIII (Winter, 1961), 466–79; Jerre Mangione, *The Dream and the Deal: The Federal Writers' Project, 1935–1943* (Boston: Little, Brown, 1972); E. Current-Garcia, *Prairie Schooner*, XII (Winter, 1938), 295–309; Ronnie W. Clayton, "A History of the Federal Writers' Project in Louisiana" (Ph.D. dissertation, Louisiana State University, 1974); Jared Putnam, "Guides to America," *Nation*, December 24, 1938, pp. 694–96.

gaged in a "process of native self-discovery." Some parts of some guides were little better than bland and censored publicity handouts by the neighborhood better business bureau. Their quality as literary art or as history depended on the quality of the people who wrote them, or the character of the state directors, some of whom were "wildly incompetent" or "paranoid," while others had the good sense to recruit talent such as John Cheever, Saul Bellow, and Nelson Algren to do the job.[17] Just as Lyle Saxon from his New Orleans office turned out a superior state guidebook and several other notable volumes on Louisiana food and folklore, Andreassen and his HRS group in Louisiana produced some of the best county inventories ever published. But just as the FWP with its guidebooks contributed little to American literature (except by providing a living for some young writers who later did publish major work), the HRS county inventories had little perceptible influence on historians, except to give some of them employment during the inventories. As it turned out, few historians would ever use the inventories before World War II ended the uncompleted HRS program.

In 1939, as Evans and Andreassen focused their own attention, if not that of the history profession, on local and county archives, they were more concerned with the ongoing day-to-day administration of the HRS than with the future use scholars might make of their work. The job at hand was sufficient preoccupation for them. Early in 1939 the administration of the HRS underwent a change in nomenclature and, a few months later, in basic structure. Effective April 15, 1939, the WPA's Division of Women's and Professional Projects, to which the HRS belonged, became the Division of Professional and Service Projects. At the same time several other WPA offices were placed in this newly named division, notably the offices of Education Projects and Recreation Projects. As Florence Kerr, director of the new DPSP expressed it, this combined in one administration all WPA projects in "the non-construction field." Evidently, it was this occupational (or professional) distinction, rather than a feminist bias, that lay behind

17. Robert Cantwell, "America and the Writers' Project," *New Republic*, April 26, 1939, pp. 323–25; Harold Rosenberg, "Anyone Who Could Write English," *New Yorker*, January 20, 1973, pp. 99–102; Malcolm Cowley, "Federal Writers' Project," *New Republic*, October 21, 1972, pp. 23–26.

the disappearance of the word *women* from the division's title. Florence Kerr had become head of the DWPP in January, 1939, succeeding another woman in the job, and she remained as head of the new DPSP. At least in Louisiana, women were as prominent on the HRS rolls after the change as before it, and if anything, they outnumbered men in both skilled and unskilled positions. Andreassen seemed to make no deliberate distinction between sexes when he appointed foremen and editors and assigned chores. At the end of 1938 the imprints supervisor in Louisiana (Burnis Walker, male) had thirty-seven workers in his charge. In the Civil District Court building in New Orleans, foreman Robert Clark directed the work of four women and one man. In the state library, Margaret K. Ward was foreman to a three-man work crew. In Howard Memorial Library, foreman Charles R. Riley headed a group of twelve women and one man, the latter assigned the task of "getting the books from the shelves."[18]

If sex discrimination in Louisiana was minimal, race discrimination was not, unless it be argued that the lack of skill and not race deprived Louisiana blacks of employment on the HRS. Supervisor Vergil Bedsole reported in February, 1939, that "Negro participation in the program of the Louisiana Historical Records Survey is confined solely to work in Negro Church archives and associations, organizations, etc." Up to January, 1939, there were "eight Negroes assigned out of a statewide quota of 404 workers." In January, 1939, when the state quota dropped to three hundred, five blacks remained on the rolls. All of these had some college education, all of them contacted "pastors and church officials for information concerning the Church history and Church archives." Their foreman (white, male), who also had eight white workers in his unit, reported that the "quality of work" by the blacks was "inferior" to that of the whites, but to Bedsole this was no cause for concern. He felt that although it was "very difficult for the Negroes to make an inventory of the records of a large church, most of the Negro churches are small and possess few records [and so] the making of a survey is far simpler than that of white churches."[19]

18. Kerr to Regional Directors, March 7, 1939, memo, Andreassen to Evans, December 7, 1938, both in 43-11, LHRS.
19. Bedsole to Evans, February 10, 1939, in *ibid.*

In 1939 this condescension and discrimination evoked little complaint from black or white. Protests by a few blacks in Louisiana and support for them from Washington had produced a Dillard Writers' Project within the LWP, which gathered enough material for a history, "The Negro in Louisiana." The manuscript of 1,128 pages and the accompanying material were deposited at Dillard University in 1942 but subsequently disappeared. But criticisms of the HRS from without, like protests and concerns expressed from within the Survey, focused on other shortcomings or problems. A major concern that arose in the summer of 1939 was the very survival of the HRS and the fate of its projected but still unfinished program. On June 30, 1939, by act of Congress, the HRS (and all of Federal One) lost the WPA as a sponsor. Since its inception in 1935, the Four Arts Program had been financed by the WPA. The HRS from time to time had received infinitesimal amounts of support from other sponsors. In Louisiana, for example, the LSU Department of Archives had contributed $110.50 between July 1 and December 31, 1937, for stencils, paper, and mimeograph machines used to print inventories. A series of laws and administrative changes in 1939 made the states and not the federal government sponsor of the HRS and the writers, artists, and musicians programs, though the word *sponsor* took on varied and even paradoxical meanings. The WPA (renamed the Work Projects Administration) continued to subsidize up to 75 percent of all HRS costs, chiefly for labor. The sponsor in each state now controlled the state HRS program but put up only 25 percent of the costs, mostly for printing and binding.[20]

From their beginning each of the Four Arts programs had come under fire from critics—ranging from those who harped on anything the New Deal did, to those who were horrified to see the government supporting artists and other parasites simply to paint or write or act, to those who saw the entire Four Arts program as a Communist plot.

20. Ronnie W. Clayton, "The Federal Writers' Project for Blacks in Louisiana," *Louisiana History*, XIX (Summer, 1977), 327–35. *Cf.* Jerah Johnson, "Marcus B. Christian and the WPA History of Black People in Louisiana," *Louisiana History*, XX (Winter, 1979), 113–15, which notes the location and availability of this material. See William F. McDonald, *Federal Relief Administration and the Arts* (Columbus: Ohio State University Press, 1969), 309–337, for a detailed discussion of the multitudinous meanings of "sponsorship" by the states after June, 1939.

The HRS had suffered far less criticism than the writers, artists, actors and musicians had, but as part of Federal One, the Survey lost its federal sponsor when the other agencies did. And that loss was due primarily, though not solely, to the "spectre of communism" that certain congressmen found in Federal One. Late in 1938 Congressman Martin Dies of Texas, chairman of the newly created House Committee on Un-American Activities, led his committee into a headlong assault on the "communist menace" he saw threatening the country. Although witnesses testifying before his committee tried to associate the Boy Scouts of America and the Campfire Girls (among other groups) with Communist subversion, it was the "intellectuals" in the FWP and especially the Federal Theatre who attracted much of the committee's attention, especially that of committee member J. Parnell Thomas of New Jersey.[21]

While the Federal Bureau of Investigation checked on the Marxist sympathies of executives on the Oklahoma Writers' Project, Trotskyite factions in the California project feuded with Stalinists, and the "predominantly Communist" Boston Writers' Union disrupted the program in Massachusetts, Congressman Thomas began holding hearings in New York City in mid-1938. Thomas, who earlier had declared that the Federal Theatre was "serving as a branch of the communistic organization [and as] one more link in the vast . . . New Deal propaganda machine," announced that the FWP was "worse than the Federal Theatre Project and a hotbed of Communism."[22] Later, in Washington hearings, the full Dies committee chose not to distinguish degrees of corruption and subversion—the Federal Theatre and the Federal Writers' Project were both contaminated with pinkos, fellow travelers, and Communists.

The hearings, the publicity, and the accusations that the Dies committee staged and provoked by themselves might not have closed down Federal One. But by 1939, the New Deal relief program was already in trouble. The 1937 recession, Roosevelt's attempt to pack the

21. William E. Leuchtenburg, *Franklin D. Roosevelt and the New Deal, 1932–1940* (New York: Harper and Row, 1963), 280–81; Penkower, *The Federal Writers' Project*, 181ff.; Jane DeHart Mathews, *The Federal Theatre, 1935–1939: Plays, Relief, and Politics* (Princeton: Princeton University Press, 1967), 198ff.

22. Penkower, *Federal Writers' Project*, 181ff; Thomas quoted in Mathews, *The Federal Theatre*, 199, and Penkower, *Federal Writers' Project*, 194.

Supreme Court, and the election of New Deal opponents to Congress in 1938, added to the conventional charges of WPA boondoggling and of Federal One as a sanctuary for idle actors and writers, be they Red or not—all this provoked a sharp reaction against the New Deal's patronage of the Four Arts Program. The Federal Theatre was abolished, and the other arts projects now became state programs. Each arts program in each state had to find an official sponsor in state government or an agency thereof. In the name of the state, the new sponsor now directed the state program. As the authoritative study on the Four Arts program expresses it: "There were now as many official projects as there were states operating projects in one or more of the arts programs."[23]

All of these projects together now bore the name WPA Arts Program, broken down into the WPA Art Program, WPA Music Program, WPA Writers' Program, and WPA Historical Records Program. The national directors of these programs remained in office in Washington and tried to direct and coordinate the work of each state office, but "when they lost control of the purse, they lost . . . authority." Given his performance as HRS director, Luther Evans might well have retained at least a moral if not a fiscal authority, but he resigned his post in November, 1939, and took another one at the Library of Congress, where he advanced to the top, becoming Librarian of Congress in June, 1945. Evans had anticipated the demise of Federal One. He had never favored a permanent Four Arts program and had from its inception thought of the HRS as an emergency agency, designed to carry out a survey that, once done, could mark the end of the HRS. In fact, the Survey's work was not finished when Evans resigned. He was replaced by Sargent Child, who had been with the WPA since its inception and Evans' assistant since the creation of the HRS in February, 1936. A native of Vermont, Child had degrees from Amherst and Columbia, had done graduate work at New York University and the University of Berlin, and had studied natural science at the Smithsonian Institution. He was interested in Latin American exploration, had helped to organize expeditions to Ecuador and Peru, and was in the party that discovered the source of the Orinoco River in 1931.

23. McDonald, *Federal Relief and the Arts*, 314.

Child had come to Washington in 1934 to work for the Press Intelligence Service and afterward had worked for the Federal Housing Authority.[24] He was as capable as Evans to direct the work to completion, insofar as any national director could still do it, and the HRS made an easy transition to state sponsorship. Evans could not have foreseen that World War II would interfere and bring a finish instead of a fulfillment to the Arts Program.

What was foreseeable to him in June, 1939, was the decision by Congress on August 31 to throw the arts projects back to the states. And three months before the bill to abolish the HRS as a federal project passed Congress, Evans had his regional supervisors out looking for local sponsors for each state Survey. These were far easier to find than were sponsors for music and art projects. In 1939 few states had public agencies with the authority or funds to sponsor such programs, but almost every state had an official archival program with jurisdiction and money enough to become sponsor of the state survey. Also, as William F. McDonald points out, "There was an official cast to the work of the H.R.S. that made it politically respectable." The HRS had always had its troubles with suspicious custodians and politically sensitive clerks, but compared to the radical image that the FWP and Federal Theatre had projected, the HRS was 100 percent American and engaged with a classic all-American theme: law and politics at the grassroots. The HRS quickly gained a sponsor in every state, including two in California, where a northern and a southern district had been formed, one in New York City, and one in the District of Columbia, each seen as a state in the Survey's table of organization. Sargent Child reported that "in the great majority of cases the projects did not cease functioning a single day."[25]

24. *Ibid.*, 321; WPA News Release, March 12, 1940 (typescript in "Personnel Data," Box 244, NA/HRS). See also McDonald, *Federal Relief and the Arts*, 772.

25. Sargent B. Child, "Status and Plans for Completion of the Inventories of the Historical Records Survey," June, 1940 (copy in 43-12, LHRS); McDonald, *Federal Relief and the Arts*, 786.

V. *Finishing Up and Closing Down*

Louisiana moved easily from federal to state sponsorship. On September 1, 1939, the Louisiana HRS acquired the LSU Department of Archives as sponsor and rapidly thereafter picked up what Andreassen described as "many contributing co-sponsors," among them the police jury in virtually every parish and a scattering of civic and historical bodies in New Orleans. Louisiana was hardly unique in having the state university's department of archives as sponsor. In most states, it was the state university, the state archives, or a state-supported historical association that wound up as sponsor.[1] Since the Department of Archives had been sponsor of a sort to the HRS from the beginning, its new status marked, for the most part, simply a formal adherence to the 1939 reorganization act. Other changes in administration and nomenclature were likewise more formal than substantial: the Louisiana HRS, already placed in the Research and Records Section of the WPA's Division of Professional and Service Projects, on March 2, 1940, became the Louisiana Statewide Records Project. Also, besides changing its name, the Louisiana HRS changed the location of its vital New Orleans office, which moved in September, 1939, to the third floor of the old Criminal Court Building at Saratoga and Tulane Street, in New Orleans. While this change in sponsors, ad-

---

1. John Andreassen, "Report on the Louisiana Statewide Records Project and Historical Records Survey, May 1, 1940" (typescript in 43-11), Andreassen to James A. McMillen (Director of Libraries, LSU), September 1, 1939, Andreassen to Luther Evans, September 6, 1939, both in 43-12, all in HRS Papers, Department of Archives, Louisiana State University Library, Baton Rouge, hereinafter cited as LHRS. See list of sponsors in "Progress Report," March 4, 1940, in Progress Reports, Box 212, Record Group No. 69, (Work Projects Administration), National Archives, hereinafter cited as NA/HRS.

ministrative channels, name, and address took place, the work of the survey went on with little if any break in the routine and schedules that Andreassen and staff had established before Congress abolished Federal One.

On September 1, as the HRS picked up its sponsor at LSU, Andreassen listed the survey's current activity: with twelve volumes of inventories already published, inventories were underway in sixty-one of the sixty-four parishes; preliminary inventories were "practically complete" for the secretary of state's office and for New Orleans courts; police jury minutes were being transcribed in forty-nine parishes; work in church archives was "progressing," and inventories of Jewish synagogues in Louisiana were "completed"; work on the Middle America project—inventories of archaeological and historical manuscripts and artifacts at Tulane—was "in process," as was a compilation of laws regarding parish boundaries.[2]

There were some 300 workers on the payroll. During the following nine months that figure rose to over 500, and on May 1, 1940, it stood at 526. By then, Andreassen had constructed a statewide administrative scheme, in which field workers were under immediate direction of field unit foremen, who in turn were answerable to HRS district supervisors in each of six cities—New Orleans, Baton Rouge, Lake Charles, Alexandria, Shreveport and Monroe. The six district supervisors received technical aid from a staff of consultants in the New Orleans state office. Their aid consisted mostly of editing reports from the field and preparing them for publication as inventories. Andreassen, never reluctant to deplore shoddy work or to criticize personnel in Louisiana as well as in Region III, thought well of his supervisory staff. The reorganization bill of June, 1939, had required that all project employees (excepting veterans and certain supervisors) working on the WPA for eighteen consecutive months be released for at least one month. This was designed to encourage workers to find private jobs and thereby either reduce public relief spending or at least give another unemployed worker a turn at the WPA trough. But the ruling affected HRS efficiency more than economy. It forced workers off the rolls just about the time they had learned their job; and they were

2. Andreassen to Luther Evans, September 6, 1939, in 43-12, LHRS.

promptly replaced by new entrants on the payroll or themselves came back after the one-month interlude. Louisiana did not suffer from the ruling, either because most released workers came back to the job or because Andreassen (and Evans) had established a working procedure that new employees quickly learned. Andreassen reported in May, 1940, that the eighteen-month clause had "not seriously affected project operations since a training program is constantly underway." In fact, he claimed that "in the past three years we have never operated with better worker talent than . . . now."[3]

Whatever their talent, Andreassen's workers and staff by May, 1940, had "entered" all but two Louisiana parishes, had published inventories for twelve of them, and were rechecking or editing eighteen more. In addition, Andreassen had released two publications that he described as "incidental to the parish inventories"—*Judicial and Congressional District Boundary Law in Louisiana* and *County-Parish Boundaries in Louisiana*. One by one as they were published, Andreassen distributed all the parish inventories to the clerk of court in each of the sixty-four parishes in the state. Thereby, in theory, each clerk's office would eventually contain what Andreassen called a "catalog" of the archives in each parish courthouse. Anyone could "go to his courthouse to determine whether it will be worth while to check certain records in a neighboring parish." To Andreassen, as to Evans, the value of the inventories to "the student of history and local government" was "obvious." This was one reason why Andreassen distributed the inventories—he thought they were useful. He also distributed them because he was required to do so. In the early days of the HRS, Evans had drawn up a list of recipients for county inventories and for all other HRS publications. In May, 1940, Florence Kerr's office in the Division of Professional and Service Projects sent out an updated distribution list, one that suggests the same conception that Evans had earlier formed about the value of the HRS to historians and other citizens probing into the records of American politics, state and local,

3. William F. McDonald, *Federal Relief Administration and the Arts* (Columbus: Ohio State University Press, 1969), 337–38, 778, discusses the ruling and points out that, while it affected the HRS "no less than other white-collar projects," the HRS was "better situated than the more professional Music Project, where the loss of even one key person might wreck the integrity of an orchestra or band"; Andreassen, "Report on Louisiana Statewide Records Project."

past and present. In state after state, libraries and archives and historical societies ranging from the Alabama Department of Archives and History, to the Newberry Library in Chicago, to the Minnesota Historical Society, to the San Jacinto Museum in Texas were the recipients of HRS inventories. In Louisiana, LSU and Tulane were supposed to receive copies of all HRS publications, though like a great many depositories, neither school ever received anything close to the total published.[4]

In continuing to stress parish inventories during the months following the demise of Federal One, Andreassen and the Louisiana HRS did just what surveys in the rest of the nation did. Also, like most other state units, Louisiana stepped up publication of inventories from other archives besides the traditional county holdings. As soon as Congress began to consider cutting back support for Federal One, historians and other supporters of the county inventories began to fret about getting them done. As Robert Binkley, one of the key figures in the very conception of the HRS, expressed it, it was always "an essential part of the plan that these inventories be compiled according to a common standard and with every county and town in the country covered." Binkley feared that the end of federal control may mark the end of the HRS and the inventory of county archives. "If it is left to some states to inventory their archives and to others to refrain," the HRS county inventories would "be like sets of encyclopaedias from which certain volumes are missing." Evans' successor, Sargent Child, promised to continue the emphasis on county and town but admitted one difficulty, "We must defer . . . to the wishes of the fifty-one sponsors and the thousand and one co-sponsors when they ask us to issue inventories of state and municipal records."[5]

If pressure from state sponsors determined in some measure what

4. Evans to State Directors, HRS, May 19, 1938, in 43-11, Florence Kerr to State WPA Administrators, May 24, 1940, in 43-12, both in LHRS. In May, 1940, registrar of manuscripts Lewis E. Newman wrote to several HRS units that had failed to mail their publications to LSU. In September, 1941, Newman compiled a fourteen-page list of HRS items still missing from forty-two states, including seven titles from Louisiana. See "Andreassen Correspondence, 1940–41," in 43-12, LHRS.

5. Robert Binkley to Edwin Davis, May 23, 1939, in "Papers by HRS Personnel," Sargent B. Child, "Status and Plans for Completion of the Inventories of the Historical Records Survey," June, 1940 (copy), both in 43-12, LHRS.

the HRS published in Louisiana, it was never at the expense of county (parish) inventories; and Louisiana's increased attention to state, church, municipal, and other holdings after 1939 was less a response to sponsor's pressure than it was simply completion of work begun in the earliest days of the HRS. It may not be a coincidence that the Louisiana HRS, which transcribed and published twenty-four volumes of police jury minutes, listed forty-eight police juries among its sixty cosponsors in May, 1940. Yet Andreassen's field workers had begun their transcriptions well before the reorganization bill of 1939 forced the HRS to find state sponsors. By May, 1940, when Andreassen listed the offices and archives currently undergoing inventory, he began with a report on the parishes but then listed six other kinds of inventories and indices underway or already done: those in state, municipal, and church archives and newspaper, manuscript, and American imprint inventories. Even so, the focus was still on the county. Among the twenty-eight titles already published by May, twelve were inventories of parish archives and six were transcriptions of police jury minutes. Of the one hundred or so items the state HRS eventually published, over half were inventories of parish archives or transcriptions of police jury minutes.[6]

While Andreassen was expanding the inventories (though retaining the old emphasis on the parish), his own interests were expanding, too. In February, 1940, Luther Evans, resigning as HRS director, nominated Andreassen as his successor. Andreassen went to Washington for an interview and meantime asked for letters of recommendation from various historians, archivists, and HRS personnel. Florence Kerr, director of the Professional and Service Division, chose Sargent Child for the job, and Andreassen, who would eventually go to Washington in another capacity, went on with the work in Louisiana.[7]

By October, 1940, he had come up with an advisory committee, a group of "professional men" around the state, who offered him "comment and suggestions on given problems and proposals." As of October 4, 1940, the committee consisted of Dean H. L. Griffin, Southwestern Louisiana Institute, Lafayette; Professor Walter Prichard, LSU; Professor John S. Kendall, Tulane University; André Lafarque,

6. Andreassen, "Report on Louisiana Statewide Records Project."
7. "Andreassen Correspondence," in 43-12, LHRS.

New Orleans; Sidney A. Marchand, Donaldsonville; H. Flood Madison, Jr., and Fred Williamson, Monroe; Robert F. Kennon, Minden; Robert Dabney Calhoun, Vidalia; Elrie Robinson, Saint Francisville; and Edwin Davis, LSU. The committee was like the list of recipients of HRS publications, which Andreassen sharply increased about the same time he formed the committee, a means of stimulating support, verbal and monetary, for the HRS and of justifying the work the HRS had been doing and still had to do. Complaints had begun to surface about the lack of HRS publications. In June, 1940, Sargent Child reported a "growing insistence by scholars, public officials, and . . . the WPA in Washington and in the states" that the Survey show some published results of activity by its thousands of workers. The "scholars and officials" were not satisfied with "the fact that hundreds of thousands of record volumes in over eight thousand courthouses, city halls, town halls, historical societies, and libraries, had been sorted and arranged while reflection of all this salvage and recovery in published inventories was modest.[8] But publication took money, which now had to come from sponsors in the states. It was hard enough for some states to pay for even minimal publications, harder still to supply copies to the several hundred depositories around the country wanting to receive them. Finding funds to subsidize publications, Child admitted, was a "pressing problem."

Louisiana overcame the problem. In fact, Andreassen got publication money from sponsors more readily than he got approval from Washington for some of the state's inventories—most notably the police jury transcriptions. From the time the state HRS first began to transcribe the police jury minutes, Andreassen had to explain and justify the project not to the police juries, which liked the idea, but to Washington, which did not. As Evans had conceived it, the HRS was supposed to find and salvage and index records, not literally copy and publish them. But Andreassen had good reason to transcribe the minutes and, understandably, had financial support from current police juries themselves to see the project completed, at least for their own parish. In 1940 the Saint Bernard police jury budgeted $1,200 for publication of the parish minutes, which may explain the fact that six

---

8. Child, "Status and Plans for Completion of the Inventories."

of the twenty-five volumes of transcriptions published in Louisiana were on Saint Bernard Parish. But in the fall of 1940, a year during which Louisiana published thirteen volumes of the minutes, totaling some 5,600 pages, Andreassen was "severely questioned" about the transcriptions by the newly formed National Advisory Committee of the HRS, which consisted of Sargent Child, Margaret C. Norton, John Clement, C. C. Crittenden, and the chairman, Julian P. Boyd.[9]

Andreassen wrote a memorandum spelling out his rationale for the transcriptions. He had wanted to obtain "accurate data from archival sources" for the historical and administrative essays his editors were to do for each parish inventory. He also wanted to make a thorough and accurate index of the minutes in each parish, whether he actually transcribed them or not. It would have cost too much to send a "trained historian" from New Orleans into each parish, but the field workers on the job could transcribe the minutes under the clear but detailed and rigorous rules that Andreassen supplied them with, even while they salvaged and inventoried all the parish public records found along with the police jury minutes. Editors in New Orleans could use the transcriptions for writing the introductory essays and could also index the minutes. Among all parish records, the minutes were to Andreassen the most valuable, most revealing, most worthy of preservation and of being made accessible to the public—hence their scrupulously accurate transcription from the handwritten originals and their publication. The indexes would, he thought, be especially valuable to local officials in the parishes, who could thereby find in the minutes all kinds of historical and legal information about their own parish, as governed by past juries. The parish in Louisiana, he noted, was "closer to a municipal corporation than the county in most other states." The police jury was the governing body; it ran the county through the ordinances it issued. And these ordinances were, "next to the municipal ordinances of our cities, the greatest legal no-man's land in conduct of our governmental affairs today." To provide current police juries and other interested citizens with a "preliminary control over this vast body of local law," the Louisiana HRS staff pre-

9. For various committee reports, see Box B52, American Council of Learned Society Papers, Division of Manuscripts, Library of Congress, hereinafter cited as ACLS Papers.

pared chronological lists of the police jury ordinances for each volume of minutes that the Survey published. Andreassen thought the lists might serve as basis for an eventual codification of the ordinances.[10]

As it turned out, the Louisiana HRS did not finish the transcription program that Andreassen had planned. The Survey published five volumes (plus an index) of minutes for Iberville Parish, thirteen volumes for Jefferson Parish, and six for Saint Bernard Parish. The last of these appeared in print three months after Japan's attack at Pearl Harbor. The beginning of the war was the beginning of the end for numerous New Deal agencies, among them the already fading programs for writers, artists, musicians, and the still-productive HRS. Beginning as a minor agency in the FWP, the HRS had gained an identity of its own, separate from, if associated with, the other Four Arts projects. And it had weathered the demise of Federal One more successfully than its companion agencies did, but it could not survive World War II.

Eighteen months before America went to war, historians and administrators on the HRS payroll and some who were not began trying to justify the HRS as an agency contributing to national defense. In June, 1940, one of the five subcommittees of the NAC, the Committee on an Emergency Program, drew up a "Preliminary Proposal for Utilization of the Historical Records Survey in the Event of a National Emergency." The language and tone of the report were suggestive of the solemnity and sense of national crisis already building well before Pearl Harbor. *Emergency* in the subcommittee's name referred to the danger that the United States would be drawn into World War II. The "Preliminary Proposal" began with an evaluation of the HRS, which found that it was "well organized, active, and functioning on a national scale." With its ten thousand employees it was "one of the few nation-wide projects which reaches into every state and county in the union." Its chief concern had been with the records of that union—"the spiritual, physical and material manifestation of the development of democracy in a great country." In its surveys and inventories, the HRS had trained thousands of people "in the use of our national

10. Andreassen, "Publication of Police Jury Minutes," November 4, 1940, memo, in 43-12, LHRS.

records, . . . both in the techniques of custody and protection of records, and also in their significance as the basis of a democratic culture." Through its close contacts with "local sentiment" in colleges,
fraternal orders, and churches, and among newsmen and politicians,
the HRS had "won the confidence and esteem of communities in a
way that few other projects have." If the United States went to war, it
would need a "national fact-finding agency" to assemble data from
every locality and, in turn, to disseminate information from Washington to every part of the country. The HRS had the experience, the
organization, and the will to become such a "Clearing House of Information and Service in Time of a National Emergency." It could fur-
nish birth records to draft boards so as to simplify the draft system
and materially reduce draft evasion. It could protect existing public
records that might be in danger of destruction during a war; it could
do the same for the "great masses of records" that would be created
by a war. It could even "make reports to the Federal Bureau of Investigation on Fifth Column activities discovered in localities." It could
become a propaganda agency by "sifting from the great body of records to which it has access the inspiring and needed lesson in what
American democracy means."[11]

In war, the HRS became neither fact finder, protector of records,
FBI informant, nor propagandist. Instead, it simply and quietly came
to an end in June, 1942. It did, during the two years preceding that
termination, shift its efforts more toward "national defense" while
trying to continue its original program of salvage and survey in public
records to completion. Whether in the interest of national defense or
in the interest of historical research, the HRS still looked for records.
The Survey's work in vital statistics was by 1940 doubly justified. The
New Deal, with its social legislation, had already created a need for
such statistics (as in the Social Security system), and the Selective Service Act, passed in September, 1940, sharpened the demand for data
on such fundamentals as age, sex, and citizenship.

In its last two years of existence, the Louisiana HRS reflected the
new emphasis on defense, but it also tried to finish the surveys and
inventories that it had begun in the midst of another emergency, that

11. Report of NAC subcommittee, in Box B52, ACLS Papers.

of the Great Depression. Through 1941 and well into 1942, parish inventories one by one appeared in print, as did guides to newspapers and manuscripts, police jury transcriptions, and directories and inventories of courts and churches. But alongside these traditional items appeared others that showed the newer concern over war: guides to vital statistics, a microfilm of birth records in New Orleans, and an "Inventory of the Records of World War Emergency Activities in Louisiana, 1916–1920."[12]

During its last two years the Louisiana HRS also began to publish more inventories of federal archives in the state. A project separate from the HRS, the Survey of Federal Archives, had begun operation in January, 1936, and had remained in existence until June, 1937, when the HRS began to take on its job of surveying federal records in the states as well as the state and local records that Evans had apportioned to the HRS. In July, 1941, Andreassen became supervisor of the Survey of Federal Archives in Louisiana. Through 1941 and into 1942, his staff brought to publication the modest number of inventories made of federal records in the state.[13]

In October, 1941, Andreassen resigned as HRS and SFA supervisor in Louisiana and moved to Washington to work in Florence Kerr's Division of Professional and Service Projects. Vergil Bedsole succeeded Andreassen in Louisiana, and Paul Eakin, in turn, succeeded him, as the Louisiana HRS rapidly closed down. The Department of Archives at LSU continued to publish inventories well into 1942, but these had been completed before the demise of the HRS, which occurred by WPA decree as of July 1, 1942. No funds had been appropriated for the new fiscal year that began on that date.[14]

Sargent Child in the Washington office (reduced to four persons, including a secretary, by January 1, 1942) thought that the HRS had not come to a close but rather to a temporary cessation. He talked of drawing "blueprints . . . for the future day after the war when the

12. John C. L. Andreassen, "Check List of Historical Records Survey and Survey of Federal Archives Publications for Louisiana," *Louisiana Historical Quarterly,* XXVII (April, 1944), 613–23.
13. Frances T. Bourne, "Preliminary Checklist of the Records of the Survey of Federal Archives of the Works Projects Administration, 1936–1945," June, 1944 (mimeograph copy available at the National Archives); Andreassen, "Check List."
14. "Andreassen Correspondence," in 43-12, LHRS.

survey will again be continued." It was "inconceivable" that the HRS would be "permanently discontinued," since it had been "beyond question . . . the largest project of its nature ever undertaken by any nation at any time" and had produced "a remarkably valuable result." The "momentum" it had gained during its six and one half years of existence could not be lost "even with the interruption of an earth-shaking war."[15]

The HRS never regained that momentum. Like much of the New Deal's emergency program, the HRS belonged to the depression thirties. Pearl Harbor ended the depression, ended the thirties, and ended the Historical Records Survey.

15. Sargent Child, "What Is Past Is Prologue," *American Archivist*, V (October, 1942), 217–18.

Epilogue and Retrospect

During World War II, the HRS inventories published before 1942 lay neglected on the shelves. The end of war brought neither renewal of the HRS nor utilization of the work it had done. Unused and unfinished, even that work became useless as archivists and custodians altered storage policies established for them by the HRS or lost once more the material that HRS workers had dug up from coal and garbage bins. And eventually even the HRS publications themselves were lost, literally, from some of the archives designated as HRS depositories, and, figuratively, from view by the history profession that since the turn of the century had so earnestly and piously clamored for the records that the HRS had given them.

As the HRS began to close up shop in 1942, Sargent Child took stock of its achievements. He counted a "grand total" of 1,940 HRS publications. The largest category among these was the inventory of county archives series, with 628 titles. The "field work" had been done in 90 percent of the nation's 3,066 counties, so that in addition to the published inventories, the HRS would deposit in state archives and libraries "tremendous quantities" of source materials which it had gathered but not yet published and had used in compiling the introductory essays for the inventories. The other categories had received less attention, and the published titles were fewer, though here, too, much more work was done than the publication figures indicated: 584 titles in the inventory of federal archives series; 28 inventories of state archives (a "large number" of additional titles in this series were ready for publication); 180 inventories of municipal and town archives (a number that could "only suggest what has actually been completed"); 107 calendars and guides to manuscripts; 164 volumes of church archives inventories and directories; and sundry titles and listings in the American imprints inventory, the checklists of newspapers, the annotated bibliography of American history, and the atlas of congressional votes—ambitious surveys only partially done when the HRS closed down. Child estimated that "ten times as much inventory and research material has been collected and placed in orderly arrangement as has been published."[1]

Child marveled at the potential for historians in all this: "What a vast amount of material awaits editing and publishing! Can anything be done about it?" As it turned out, not much was done at all. These tons of HRS material, published and unpublished alike, received the same treatment that the public records it surveyed had received before the HRS set out to salvage them—neglect and destruction. Some fifteen years after World War II, Leonard Rapport of the National Archives staff set out to locate the records of the HRS. He found more dead ends and (for an archivist) horror stories than he did records. In October, 1950, in Connecticut, 108 cases of that state's HRS records deposited at Yale in 1942 were loaded on a truck bound for the Connecticut State Library, but the library had no record and the library staff had no recollection that the 108 cases were ever delivered. Like most of those in New England and states elsewhere, Connecticut's records just disappeared. In Maine, their disappearance was at least recorded (or remembered): when no library in Maine would accept HRS material for storage, it was "dumped from a wharf into Casco Bay."[2]

One can and should deplore this treatment of HRS material. And there is irony worth noting, as well: that archivists and historians have treated the records of the HRS the same way custodians and public officials had for generations treated the records the HRS set out to salvage. Contrary to the plans of historians ranging from Herbert Levi Osgood in 1901 to Robert C. Binkley and Luther H. Evans in the 1930s, from archivist Robert T. Swan in Massachusetts in the 1890s

---

1. Sargent Child, "What Is Past Is Prologue," *American Archivist*, V (October, 1942), 217–18.
2. Leonard Rapport, "Dumped from a Wharf into Casco Bay: The Historical Records Survey Revisited," *American Archivist*, XXXVII (April, 1974), 201–210.

to HRS supervisor John Andreassen in Louisiana in the 1930s, neither historians nor lawyers nor genealogists nor public officials have ever made use of the records that the HRS salvaged or the inventories of those records they so carefully compiled. And yet there is at least one qualification, one explanation, if not justification, to add—that the primary purpose of the HRS, as Leonard Rapport has noted, "was not to survey records but to give work to the unemployed."[3] Whatever the fate of the HRS at the hands of historians and the "public officials" whom Evans thought would exploit its inventories, the HRS should be judged primarily for what it was. It was an emergency relief program conceived during the Depression for white-collar Americans, who were to receive federal patronage (read minimum wages) for doing work that was at the least a clerical chore, at best a creative art.

The history of the Historical Records Survey demonstrates that in the name of work relief, the federal government could serve as patron to an organization of clerks and scholars who, in return for the subsistence the nation's government supplied them, made available to that nation a storehouse of archival treasures. That the storehouse later suffered neglect and decay is an adverse judgment on a later generation. It should detract not at all from the achievements of the HRS from 1936 to 1942, at least not in Louisiana, where the HRS did its job well.

---

3. *Ibid.*

Appendix

From the *St. Bernard Parish Inventory*, published in December, 1938, I have selected for reproduction here the following items:

Cover

Foreword

Preface

Table of Contents

Historical Sketch (of the parish)

Maps of Evolution of Boundaries of Saint Bernard Parish

Essay entitled "Governmental Organization and Records System"

Essay entitled "Housing, Care, and Accessibility of the Records"

List of Abbreviations, Symbols, and Explanatory Notes

Essay entitled "Police Jury"

Essay entitled "Notaries Public" and six pages of entries made for records in the Clerk of Court Office

Essay entitled "Clerk of Court" and two pages of entries made for records in this office

Essay entitled "Sheriff" and two pages of entries made for records in this office

Inventory of the Parish Archives of Louisiana

•

No. 44. ST. BERNARD PARISH (ST. BERNARD)

•

Prepared by

THE HISTORICAL RECORDS SURVEY
DIVISION OF WOMEN'S AND PROFESSIONAL PROJECTS
WORKS PROGRESS ADMINISTRATION

•

THE DEPARTMENT OF ARCHIVES
LOUISIANA STATE UNIVERSITY

FOREWORD

The Inventory of the Parish Archives of Louisiana is one of a number of bibliographies of historical materials prepared throughout the United States by workers on the Historical Records Survey of the Works Progress Administration. The publication herewith presented, an inventory of the archives of Saint Bernard Parish, is number 44 of the Louisiana series.

The Historical Records Survey was undertaken in the winter of 1935-36 for the purpose of providing useful employment to needy unemployed historians, lawyers, teachers, and research and clerical workers. In carrying out this objective, the project was organized to compile inventories of historical materials, particularly the unpublished government documents and records which are basic in the administration of local government, and which provide invaluable data for students of political, economic, and social history. The archival guide herewith presented is intended to meet the requirements of day-to-day administration by the officials of the county (parish), and also the needs of lawyers, business men and other citizens who require facts from the public records for the proper conduct of their affairs. The volume is so designed that it can be used by the historian in his research in unprinted sources in the same way he uses the library card catalog for printed sources.

The inventories produced by the Historical Records Survey attempt to do more than give merely a list of records - they attempt further to sketch in the historical background of the county or other unit of government, and to describe precisely and in detail the organization and functions of the government agencies whose records they list. The county (parish), town, and other local inventories for the entire country will, when completed, constitute an encyclopedia of local government as well as a bibliography of local archives.

The successful conclusion of the work of the Historical Records Survey, even in a single county (parish), would not be possible without the support of public officials, historical and legal specialists, and many other groups in the community. Their cooperation is gratefully acknowledged.

The Survey was organized and has been directed by Luther H. Evans, and operates as a nation-wide project in the Division of Women's and Professional Projects, of which Mrs. Ellen S. Woodward, Assistant Administrator, is in charge.

HARRY L. HOPKINS
Administrator

PREFACE

In Louisiana the Historical Records Survey began operation in March
1936, under the supervision of Lyle Saxon, State Director of the Writers'
Project, who acted as State Director of the Historical Records Survey.
In the first W. P. A. district of Louisiana, the Survey was operated a-
part from the Writers' Project from the beginning. In the third W. P. A.
district, the survey was under the direction of the district supervisor
of the Writers' Project until July 1936, when a separate supervisor was
appointed. In November 1936, the Survey became an independent part of
Federal Project No. 1, but its administration and operation in Louisiana
remained unchanged. On March 10, 1937, John C. L. Andreassen became
State Director of the Historical Records Survey. Mr. Saxon continued as
State Director of the Writers' Project.

The objective of the survey in Louisiana has been the preparation
of complete inventories of the records of the state and of each parish,
municipality and other local governmental unit. Although a condensed
form of entry is used, information is given as to the limiting dates of
all extant records, the contents of the individual series, and the location of the records in the new state capitol, parish courthouses, or
other depositories. The record titles are arranged under the office of
origin and by subject; in the index, they are arranged alphabetically
but with cross references. Preceding the record entries for each office is a brief statement on the history, functions, and records of the
office.

The Inventory of Parish Archives in Louisiana will, when completed,
consist of a separate number for each parish in the state. Each unit of
the series is numbered according to its respective position in the alphabetical list of parishes. Thus the inventory herewith presented for
Saint Bernard Parish is No. 44. The inventory of the state archives and
of municipal and other local records will constitute separate publications.

In this the sixth parish inventory prepared for publication, perti-
nent legal citations have been given in the office essays. Special legislation relating to Saint Bernard Parish has been fully canvassed.

The survey in Saint Bernard Parish was started on October 19, 1936
and completed October 27, 1936. The field inventory was re-checked with
the records between April 13, and April 29, 1937. This draft received a
further re-check during June and October 1938. For the completeness and
accuracy of the inventory the parish workers are responsible. The editorial staff under Mr. George Sturgis contributed the legal histories
and did the final editing.

This unit of the Inventory of Parish Archives is being issued in
mimeographed form by the Department of Archives, Louisiana State University, for free distribution to state and local public officials and libraries in Louisiana, and to a limited number of libraries and governmental agencies outside the state. Requests for information concerning

particular units of the <u>Inventory</u> should be addressed to the State Director, or to Dr. Edwin Adams Davis, Archivist, Department of Archives and Manuscripts, Louisiana State University.

The limited number of copies of this and succeeding inventories has made essential a planned distribution of these volumes. Each Clerk of Court and Ex officio Recorder has received a copy of the Saint Charles, Lafayette, Calcasieu, Allen and Natchitoches inventories. It is hoped that the state-wide series of 64 volumes will eventually find safe deposit in these 64 widely distributed depositories.

General regulations and procedures applicable to all project units in the forty-eight states have been followed in Louisiana. The officials of W. P. A. in Louisiana have always given the project cordial support and assistance. Appreciation for the interest and cooperation of Saint Bernard Parish officials in our undertaking must be mentioned.

The State Director, John C. L. Andreassen, has for some months served as acting Regional Supervisor for the project in eleven southern states. He read the final draft before publication.

Vergil L. Bedsole
Assistant State Supervisor
Historical Records Survey

620 Canal Bank Building
New Orleans, Louisiana
December 1938

TABLE OF CONTENTS

A. St. Bernard Parish and its Records System

- 2 -

Table of Contents

(First entry, p. 44)

1. HISTORICAL SKETCH

St. Bernard Parish is closely connected with New Orleans both historically and economically. It was in St. Bernard that the British in 1699 were turned back in their first attempt to colonize the Mississippi Valley, and 116 years later met their defeat at the hands of Andrew Jackson in the Battle of New Orleans. Economically, the two parishes have been equally interdependent. New Orleans of the 1720's was only a small post surrounded by swamps, with no land for agriculture. To supply the needs of the population, plantations were established on the river below the town in what is now St. Bernard Parish. Today, from this fertile land still comes a great part of the produce for the markets of New Orleans.[1] St. Bernard, an unincorporated town, has been the seat of government most of the time since the organization of the parish in 1807.

France claimed the Mississippi Valley by right of La Salle's voyages between 1682 and 1687, but took no immediate steps to colonize.[2] In 1699 Iberville backed discovery with settlement by founding the post at Biloxi. This proved fortunate for France.[3] When Iberville returned to France in 1700, his brother, Bienville, set out on another journey of exploration on the Mississippi River, and at a point twelve miles below the site of New Orleans, met an English ship. Stopped and questioned by Bienville, the captain was reported to have said that he was looking for the Mississippi, which the English had discovered and taken possession of fifty years before ("les Anglois avoient descouvert et pris possession il y avoit cinquants annees"). When Bienville replied that the French had made settlements and were in a position to defend them, the British captain turned back down stream. It is from this incident that the place of meeting, now near the boundary line between St. Bernard and Plaquemines, was called English Turn, which name it still bears.[4] This was England's last attempt at active colonization, although by the Treaty of Paris in 1763, she received the part of Louisiana called West Florida.[5]

1. Henry E. Chambers, A History of Louisiana, Chicago and New York, 1925, 3 vols., I, pp. 105-113; John D. Klorer (ed.), The New Louisiana, New Orleans, 1936, p. 123.
2. Chambers, op. cit., I, pp. 29-44; B. F. French (comp.), Historical Collections of Louisiana, New York, 1846-1853, 5 vols., I, pp. 85-193; ibid., IV, pp. 83-97, 195-229.
3. B. F. French (comp.), Historical Collections of Louisiana and Florida, New York, 1869-1875, 2 vols., I, pp. 35-165.
4. French, Historical Collections of Louisiana, V. pp. 119-122.
5. French, Historical Collections of Louisiana, III, p. 17; Pierre Margry (ed.), Memoirs et Documents Pour Servir a L'Histoire des Origines Francais de Pays D'Outre Mer, 1614-1754, Paris, 1879-1888, 6 vols., IV, p. 361; ibid., V, p. 399; Amos Stoddard, Sketches, Historical and Descriptive, of Louisiana, Philadelphia, 1812, p. 28; cf., Alcee Fortier, A History of Louisiana, New York, 1904, 4 vols., I, p. 258; Chambers, op. cit., I, p. 496.

Under the French ownership the colonization of St. Bernard was confined mainly to individual plantations scattered along the natural levee
bordering the river. This region, a tongue of land lying between the
river and a bayou to the east, became known as the Terre aux Boeufs (the
Land of the Oxen) from the large numbers of wild oxen or buffalo found
there.[6]

In 1722, between New Orleans and the sea, there were no large
grants, only some small private habitations.[7] At that time the entire
district of New Orleans, which included the present parish of St. Bernard, showed men bearing arms, 229; women and girls, 169; orphans, 45;
slaves, 267. Probably the oldest grant in the parish was that given to
Celestin Chiapella and Magliore Guichard in July of 1723; but the An-
toine Phillippon claim of September 1723, later increased by other
grants to a total of 5,270 acres, was the largest single holding.[8]

Following the cession to Spain, intensive Spanish colonization began under the direction of Bernardo de Galvez. In 1778 he brought several hundred refugees from the Canary Islands at the King's expense,
gave each family land, cattle, farm implements and money for four years,
and provided a church for each settlement. The center of the colony, on
Bayou Terre aux Boeufs, he called New Galvez, but the people changed it
to San Bernardo, in honor of Galvez' name saint. During the same year
Marigny de Mandeville also imported colonists from the Canaries, whom he
settled on his concession in St. Bernard. Today, the descendents of
those early Spanish settlers are still spoken of as Islenos or Island
ers.[9]

The French population was increased by Acadian refugees, many of
whom found homes and safety in San Bernardo. By 1785 there were 756

6. Alcee Fortier, Louisiana, At-
    lanta, 1909, 3 vols., II, p.
    404.
7. French, Historical Collections
    of Louisiana, III, p. 182;
    "Louisiana in 1724, Banet's
    Report to the Company of the
    Indies, Dated Paris, December
    20, 1724," in La. Hist. Q.,
    1929, XII, p. 126; William Beer
    (ed.), Jay K. Ditchy (tr.),
    "Early Census Tables of Lou-
    isiana," in La. Hist. Q.,
    1930, XIII, p. 228.
8. Souvenir Program of St. Mau-
    rice Church Fair, St. Bernard
    Parish, New Orleans, 1912,
    pp. 28, 51.
9. J. D. B. De Bow (ed.), "The
    Early Times of Louisiana," in
    De Bow's Review, New Orleans,
    1846-1880, 43 vols., XXIV, pp.
    220, 221; Marie Louise Points,
    "The Old French Parish of St.
    Bernard," in the New Orleans
    and Louisiana Scrapbook, N. O.
    Public Library, p. 178; Sou-
    venir Program, pp. 32, 33;
    Goodspeed (comp.), Biographi-
    cal and Historical Memoirs of
    Louisiana, Chicago, 1892, 2
    vols., II, p. 197; Maps in the
    Cabildo, by Major A. La Car-
    riere La Tour, Jackson's chief
    engineer, show all these early
    plantations.

people settled here.[10] It proved excellent land for farmers. The soil, rich from many years of flooding, produced four crops in one year. At first the staple money crop was indigo, but with the importation of sugar-cane the planters found it the better paying commodity.[11] Gradually the country along the river for miles below New Orleans became so thickly settled that by 1804 it appeared, from the view on shipboard, as one continuous plantation, extensive and well populated. It was the seat of a district commandant, and a curacy, the revenue of which totaled 10,000 francs per year.[12] In the old parish register of St. Bernard may still be found the names of the early families - Estopinal, Nunez, Poydras, Marrero, Mendez, Beauregard, Villere, Livaudais, De La Crois - who played important parts in the history of the parish.[13]

This section, while not so greatly affected by the Louisiana Purchase as were some other parts of the state, must have received a few American settlers, for the population in 1810 had increased to 1,020. Since that time, the census reports of the parish present some interesting comparisons, particularly as to the relative numbers of white and colored. Whereas in 1810 there were 628 white and 392 colored, by 1840 the ratio was reversed, with 1,406 white to 2,396 colored. Each race increased proportionately until 1870, when a general decline was noted. In 1880 the population was again on the rise, with the two races almost equal in numbers. Since 1890, however, the white population has been gaining steadily, and in 1930 outnumbered the colored almost four to one (5175 to 1337). This trend in population would seem to parallel the breaking up of the very large plantations into smaller farms requiring less Negro labor, which in turn coincided with a change in agricultural products from cotton, sugar-cane and rice, to garden truck and fruits.[14]

10. John Sibley, "An Account of Louisiana," in American Register, Philadelphia, 1806-1810, 7 vols., IV, p. 92; DeBow, op. cit., p. 223.
11. Souvenir Program, p. 55.
12. James A. Robertson, Louisiana Under the Rule of Spain, France and the United States, 1785-1807, Cleveland, 1911, 2 vols., I, pp. 55, 97, 164, 222; Stoddard, op. cit., p. 161.
13. Souvenir Program, pp. 39-41.
14. Goodspeed, op. cit., p. 197; Ninth Census, The Statistics of the Population of the United States, Washington, 1872, I, pp. 34, 35; Tenth Census of the United States, 1880, Population, Washington, 1883, I, p. 394; Compendium of the Eleventh Census of 1890, Part I, Population, Washington, 1892, p. 414; Census Reports, Twelfth Census of the United States . . . Population, Part I, Washington, 1901, p. 542; Thirteenth Census of the United States, 1910, Population, II, Washington, 1913, p. 236; Fourteenth Census of the United States, . . . III, Population, Washington, 1922, p. 983; Fifteenth Census of the United States, 1930, III, Population, Washington, 1932, p. 1008; Rodger W. Shugg, "Survival of the Plantation System in Louisiana," in The Journal of Southern History, 1937, III, pp. 311-323; Robert R. Russel, "The General Effect of Slavery upon Southern Economic Progress," in The Journal of Southern History, 1938, IV, pp. 34-54.

In 1815, the plain of Chalmette, eight miles below New Orleans was the scene of the closing battle of the War of 1812, marking the end of the rivalry between the United States and Great Britain for possession of the lower Mississippi Valley. News traveled slowly in those days, so neither Andrew Jackson nor General Packenham, the British leader, knew, as they prepared for battle on December 23rd, that the Treaty of Ghent ending the war was being signed in Belgium. The English troops had come secretly through the lakes and bayous to St. Bernard, where Jackson, with a force of approximately 2,500 men, met and stopped them at Chalmette. The battle continued intermittently until January 8th. On that day Jackson attacked so vigorously that the British regiments were completely routed, and by the 20th had sailed away as secretly as they had come.[15]

In the celebration of the victory, which took place in the old Place d'Armes in New Orleans, Zoe Chalmette of St. Bernard placed a wreath of roses on Jackson's head. Chalmette Monument, which marks the battlefield, is a national park. Close by may be seen the ruins of the mansion on the De La Ronde plantation to which General Packenham was taken wounded and in which he died. Although the vestige of the house is nothing but a few crumbling red brick walls, the avenue of live oaks stretching to the river has been preserved.[16] The war, except for naval victories, had been singularly inglorious for America. It remained for Jackson to win such a decisive, if belated, victory that not only was national pride increased, but the Creoles of Louisiana, smarting over the transfer to the United States, were inspired with a sense of allegiance to their new country.

In the Civil War St. Bernard played vicariously a part of national importance. General Pierre Gustave Toutant Beauregard, a native of the parish, gave, on April 12, 1861, the order for the bombardment of Fort Sumter, which plunged the North and the South into war.[17] In the parish of St. Bernard both war and Reconstruction took heavy toll. It was under Federal control from 1862, and in 1863 was one of the thirteen Louisiana parishes in which the slaves were not freed by Lincoln's Emancipation Proclamation. During Reconstruction there were serious riots between the citizens and the Metropolitan Police stationed in St. Bernard. For the years 1869-1873 the cost of maintaining one corporal

15. Chambers, op. cit., I, pp. 528-538; James A. Padgett (ed.), "The Difficulties of Andrew Jackson in New Orleans, Including His Later Dispute with Fulwer Skipwith, as Shown by the Documents," in La. Hist. Q., 1938, XXI, pp. 367-419.
16. Souvenir Program, p. 39.
17. Nathaniel W. Stephenson, The Day of the Confederacy, New Haven, 1919, pp. 15-23; "Sketch of General Beauregard By His Son," in La. Hist. Q., 1919, II, pp. 276-281; Thomas Marshall Spaulding, "Pierre Beauregard," in Dictionary of American Biography, New York, 1928-1936, 20 vols., II, pp. 111, 112.

and fourteen patrolmen was $58,351.00.[18]

From the creation of the parish in 1807 until 1875 seven acts have been passed changing or defining the boundaries of St. Bernard. In 1809, in order to remove doubts relative to the limits of Orleans, Plaquemines and St. Bernard, the latter was defined as commencing at Delassize's plantation inclusively, and running along the settlements of the Bayou Terre aux Boeufs.[19] This was further clarified in 1811 by a slight change in wording: from "the back line of Lasie's (Delassize's) plantation, including all the settlements of Bayou Terre aux Boeufs."[20] The boundaries were enlarged in 1812 to include the plantations of Julian Poydras and V. Delassize,[21] and in 1817, to comprehend the tract situated on the left bank of the Mississippi river from Julian Poydras' plantation to the Canal des Pecheurs.[22] In 1842 the limits between Plaquemines and St. Bernard were defined as "beginning at the already established limits of Morgan and Poydras plantations on the river and following the same one league from the river, thence running a straight line to the junction of the Bayou Grove and Mandeville, thence following the middle of the Bayou Mandeville to the Lake Lerry, . . . thence running a line to the northeast part of Black Bay, and thence following the middle of Black Bay to the Chandeleur Bay."[23] The last changes, made in 1875, provided that hereafter the boundary of St. Bernard shall be from the left bank of the Mississippi River, along the lower line of the property known and used as the United States Parks, on the prolongation of the said line until it intersects the prolongation of the line of the south side of Florida Walk one of the avenues of the City of New Orleans, thence in an easterly direction to the point where the Canal des Pecheurs intersects the Bayou Bienville, thence along the south side of said bayou to the Lake Borgne, and thence along the boundaries of said parish as now established, to the left bank of said Mississippi River, where the parish of Plaquemines begins.[24]

When Mississippi was admitted as a state in 1817, the constitution of that state defined its southern boundary as eighteen miles out into the Gulf of Mexico and its western boundary as the Pearl River. With these lines in effect Mississippi would have occupied a portion of St. Bernard Parish. The supreme court of the United States ruled in the case "State of Louisiana vs. State of Mississippi," in 1905, that since the Territory of Orleans had constituted its boundary "as being the deep water sailing channel or Thalweg, emerging from the mouth of Pearl River and extending eastwardly to the north of Half Moon Island, through the Mississippi Sound and Cat Island Pass, between Cat Island and Isle a Pitre, and through Chandeleur Island Sound, northeast of the Chandeleur Islands to the Gulf of Mexico," and that since Louisiana when admitted as a state had adopted these boundaries, giving her priorty rights,

18. John Rose Ficklen, History of Reconstruction in Louisiana (through 1868), Baltimore, 1910, pp. 208-214; Fortier, History of Louisiana, IV, p. 39.

19. Or. Terr. A., 1809, XXX.
20. Or. Terr. A., 1811, XIX.
21. La. A., 1812-13, p. 138.
22. La. A., 1817, p. 166.
23. La. A., 1842, #14.
24. La. A., 1875, #54.

these would remain as they were.[25]

In 1935 there were in the parish 272 farms assessed at $876,050.[26] These figures are more impressive when it is realized that only 13 square miles of the total 617 may be classed strictly as agricultural lands. Although the parish is mainly agricultural, the twelve miles of river front and the low tax rate have attracted both industrial plants and homeseekers.

There are 544 square miles of marshes which are interesting at present from an economic standpoint because of the evidence of petroleum at great depths below the surface. A large part of St. Bernard has been under lease to oil companies for several years. Since only four wells have gone below 5,000 feet, they still hope to strike oil at greater depths.[27]

From the waters which almost surround the parish, fish and oysters valued annually at millions are shipped over the country. St. Bernard in 1933 produced four times as many oysters as any other parish in the entire state. From the marshes come mink and muskrat furs.[28]

In 1927, St. Bernard came into national prominence when New Orleans was threatened by the flood waters of the Mississippi River. To insure the safety of the city, Governor O. H. Simpson ordered the Caernarvon levee, a short distance below Poydras, to be cut in order to effect a spillway. Residents were removed from the danger zone by the National Guard and Red Cross workers and on April 29th state engineers blasted away sections of the levee.[30] Within the next few years claims for damages to property amounting to $4,177,631, were settled by the Orleans Levee Board, which amount the Board collected from the government in 1931.[31] To prevent a recurrence of such floods in the lower Mississippi Valley, the Bonnet Carre Spillway was built thirty miles above New Orleans. It was opened for the first time in 1937, and successfully carried the high waters through Lake Pontchartrain to the Gulf.

---

25. Supreme Court Reporter, October Term 1905, XXVI (202 U. S. 1.), pp. 408-425.
26. United States Census of Agriculture, 1935, 2 vols., I, pp. 698-700.
27. Department of Conservation, Geological Bulletin #8, Lower Mississippi River Delta, Reports on the Geology of Plaquemines and St. Bernard Parishes, New Orleans, 1936, pp. 15, 276.
28. Klorer, op. cit., p. 123; J. W. Bateman, Director, Annual Report of Agricultural Ex-

tension Work in Louisiana, Baton Rouge, 1935, p. 132; Eleventh Report of the Department of Conservation, State of Louisiana, 1932-1933, New Orleans, p. 235; Souvenir Program, pp. 14, 15, 55-57.
29. Department of Conservation, op. cit., pp. 17, 26; The Times-Picayune, New Orleans, April 30, 1927, p. 1.
30. Times-Picayune, April 29, 1927, pp. 1, 10.
31. Times-Picayune, June 21, 1931, p. 1.

MAPS OF EVOLUTION OF BOUNDARIES OF
SAINT BERNARD PARISH*

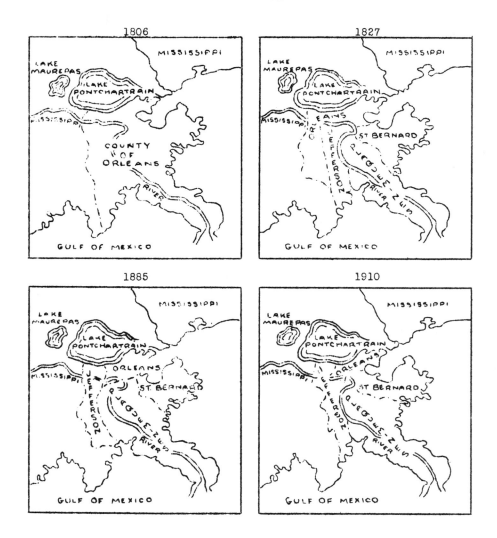

*These maps were drawn from the following maps: Louisiana, S. Lewis and H. S. Tanner, 1806; Louisiana, Mississippi, and Alabama, pub. by A. Finlay, 1827; State of Louisiana, Bureau of Immigration, 1855; all located in the Louisiana State Library, Pontalba Building, St. Ann St. For the acts of the legislature consulted in this drawing, see footnotes 19-24, p. 7.

2. GOVERNMENTAL ORGANIZATION AND RECORDS SYSTEM

The development of the system of local government in Louisiana has been strongly influenced by the cultural, religious and political background of the French and Spaniards by whom it was settled. The purchase of Louisiana resulted naturally in the introduction of Anglo-Saxon political conceptions. Since these differed from those held by the bulk of the inhabitants, there arose a certain conflict of ideas. In the realm of local affairs, compromise between the two conflicting political conceptions has resulted in the present parochial government.

The area included in the French Louisiana had not been precisely defined, and when ceded to Spain became a part of the Spanish dominion extending from Florida to California. After the Louisiana Purchase, Congress set apart from this province the Territory of Orleans, which was described as being "that portion of country ceded by France to the United States under the name of Louisiana which lies south of the Mississippi Territory and of an eastern and western line, to commence at the Mississippi River at the 33° of north latitude, and to extend to the western boundary of said cession . . ."[1] The territory was divided in 1805 into twelve counties[2] which, however, were discarded, for purposes of local government, two years later and nineteen civil parishes created in their stead.[3] The Constitution of 1812, under which Louisiana was admitted as a state, defined the limits of the state precisely. The eastern boundary was the Mississippi and Iberville rivers and lakes Maurepas and Pontchartrain, and the western boundary a line drawn up the middle of the Sabine River to the intersection with the 32° north latitude, thence north to the 33° and then along that parallel to the Mississippi River.[4]

In the meantime, however, the West Florida Revolution had resulted in an ordinance of Dec. 7, 1810 claiming the land south of the Mississippi Territory and extending eastward to the River Perdido as a county of Orleans Territory, under the name of Feliciana County.[5] This action was ratified in part, in 1812, by an act of Congress, which added to the state of Louisiana all of that region which lay west of the Pearl River.[6]

---

1. Acts of the 8th U. S. Congress, First Session, app. Mar. 26, 1804, in Francis Newton Thorpe, American Charters Constitutions and Organic Laws, Washington, 1909, 7 vols., III, p. 1364.
2. Or. Terr. A., 1805, XXV.
3. Or. Terr. A., 1807, I.
4. Const., 1812, preamble.
5. Ordinance, p. 210 in Or. Terr. Acts of 1810. On Dec. 22 another ordinance divided Feliciana County into four parishes; East Baton Rouge, Feliciana, St. Helena, and St. Tammany; cf. Ordinance, p. 210

in Or. Terr. Acts of 1810. An ordinance of Jan. 4, 1811 added the parishes of Biloxi and Pascagoula; cf. Ordinance p. 214 in Or. Terr. Acts of 1811. The boundaries of all six of these parishes were defined in 1811; cf. Or. Terr. A., 1811, XXVIII; Congress, however, by placing the Pearl River as the eastern boundary of Louisiana excluded the parishes of Biloxi and Pascagoula.

6. Acts of 12th U. S. Congress, First Session, app. Apr. 14, 1812, in Thorpe, op. cit., p. 1380.

Governmental Organization and Rec- (First entry, p. 44)
ords System

There has been a progressive division of local governmental areas into smaller units. New parishes have been created until now there are sixty-four in the state. These vary in area from 196 to 1,756 square miles; in population from 6,054 to 458,762; and in population density from 4 to 2,340 per square mile. Since only six have a population exceeding 50,000, parishes are generally rural in character.[7] All these considerations have a bearing upon the form in which the local government has been cast.

As a French colony, civil government began when Crozat was given a trade monopoly in 1712. The first steps towards the organization of local government were taken in 1721, when the territory was divided into nine districts.[8] A commandant, a judge, and a number of syndics were appointed by the governor for each district. The duties of the commandant were chiefly administrative in character; judges exercised civil and criminal jurisdiction over all cases in the district, while the syndics assisted the commandant.[9]

Although Louisiana was ceded to Spain in 1762, it was not until 1769 that the French system of government was modified and a new military and political unit created, called the Province of Louisiana. The Spanish governor, O'Reilly, divided the province into eleven districts[10] over each of which he placed a commandant having both civil and military jurisdiction. At about this time the province was divided into twenty-one ecclesiastical parishes, but, since there was a shortage of priests, only nineteen resulted.[11]

In 1795, Governor Carondelet appointed syndics, who were to be subordinate to the commandant. Their duties included the supervision of levees, roads, and drainage ditches, as well as judicial functions in minor civil matters. The syndics were stationed about nine miles apart, and this, it has been suggested, may have been the basis for the parish

7. R. L. Carleton, Local Government and Administration in Louisiana, Baton Rouge, 1935, pp. 83-88, 322, 323; Fifteenth Census of the United States, 1930, Population, III, p. 965.
8. New Orleans, Biloxi, Mobile, Alibamons, Natchez, Yazoo, Natchitoches (sometimes called Red River), Arkansas and Illinois; cf. Carleton, op. cit., pp. 14, 17, 19.
9. Carleton, op. cit., pp. 17-19.
10. These eleven districts were: Illinois, Natchitoches, 1st half of the German Coast, 2nd half of the German Coast, Pointe Coupee, Opelousas, Iberville Coast, Lafourche of Chetimachas, Kabahan-nosse, Rapides, and St. Genevieve. Including New Orleans there were really twelve districts, but New Orleans did not have a commandant.
11. Carleton, op. cit., pp. 19, 25; Alcee Fortier, History of Louisiana, II, p. 9; Robert Dabney Calhoun, "The Origin and Early Development of County-Parish Government in Louisiana," in La. Hist. Q., 1935, XVIII, pp. 56-160.

ward of later date.[12]

    After the Louisiana Purchase, the Territory of Orleans was divided
into twelve counties,[13] and the colonial commandant and syndics were replaced[14] by a county judge and justices of the peace.[15] For each county there was also appointed by the governor, a sheriff and ex officio
tax collector, a coroner, a clerk of court, and a treasurer.[16] The
county administrative body was composed of the county judge and justices
of the peace.[17] The function of recording notarial acts and other instruments was vested in the county judge.[18] The judiciary included justices of the peace with civil jurisdiction up to $50, and criminal jur-
isdiction in cases where there was a breach of the peace;[19] the county
court with civil jurisdiction up to $100, criminal jurisdiction in cases
which were not capital, and exclusive probate jurisdiction.[20] The

---

12. Carleton, op. cit., p. 26;
"Regulations to be observed
by Syndics and Alcaldes of
the jurisdiction of Baton
Rouge, 30 October 1804," in
La. Hist. Q., IX, pp. 405-410;
Amos Stoddard, Sketches, Historical and Descriptive of
Louisiana, Philadelphia,
1812, pp. 274,275; James A.
Padgett, "A Decree Issued by
the Baron of Carondelet, June
1, 1795," in La. Hist. Q.,
1937, XX, pp. 590-605.

13. The twelve counties were:
1) Orleans, composed of the
area on both sides of the
river from Balise to St.
Charles Parish and including the parish of St. Bernard and St. Louis; 2) German Coast, composed of the
parishes of St. Charles and
St. John the Baptist; 3)
Acadia, composed of the parishes of St. James and Ascension; 4) Lafourche, composed of the parish of
Assumption; 5) Iberville,
composed of the parish of
St. Gabriel and that part of
the parish of St. Bernard lying within the Territory of
Orleans; 6) Pointe Coupee,
composed of the parish of St.
Francis; 7) Concordia (de-

scribed with geographical
boundaries); 8) Ouachita, composed of the "Ouachita Settlements;" 9) Rapides, composed
of the settlements of Rapides,
Avoyelles, Catahoula, Bayous
Boeuf and Robert, and all
other settlements in the vi-
cinity; 10) Natchitoches, composed of the parish of St.
Francis; 11) Opelousas, composed of the parish of St.
Landry; 12) Attakapas, composed of St. Martin Parish.
Of these counties only the
boundaries of Concordia were
accurately defined, the remainder, except Ouachita and
Rapides, were defined in terms
of ecclesiastical parishes;
cf. Or. Terr. A., 1805, XXV,
sec. I.

14. Or. Terr. A., 1805, XLIV, sec.
I.

15. Or. Terr. A., 1805, XXV, sec.
2; ibid., XLIV, sec. 1.

16. Or. Terr. A., 1805, XXV, sec.
2; ibid., XLIII, sec. 2.

17. Or. Terr. A., 1805, XLIII,
sec. I.

18. Or. Terr. A., 1805, XLIV, sec.
I.

19. See Justices of the Peace,
p. 90.

20. See County Court, p. 71.

superior court, which went on circuit and held sessions at the county seats, was the court of last resort.[21] The county judge, in addition to his many duties, appointed constables, and, by and with the advice of the justices of the peace, imposed taxes.[22]

The county system of local government was discarded shortly.[23] Opposition to it, doubtless was caused by the decentralization of local government and by the introduction of such innovations as the use of English as the official language, and the common law procedure, which became identified in the popular mind with the county system of government.[24] Hence, in 1807, nineteen civil parishes were established.[25] Under this system a parish judge, justices of the peace, and constables were appointed for each parish.[26] This judge, with the justices of the peace and a jury of "twelve inhabitants" appointed by him, formed the policy-making and administrative body in matters of police, taxation, and internal improvements.[27] The parish judge also presided over the newly created parish and probate courts, and acted as clerk of court, sheriff, treasurer, coroner, and as tax collector.[28]

The first step to reduce the powers of the parish judge was taken in 1810, when the office of sheriff was created.[29] The following year

---

21. See Superior Court, p. 70.
22. Or. Terr. A., 1805, XXV, sec. 24; ibid., XLIII, sec. 1.
23. The county remained only for the purpose of serving as an electoral district for electing state representatives, and for the purpose of levying territorial taxes; cf. Or. Terr. A., 1807, I, sec. 32.
24. Cf. Carleton, op. cit., p. 30.
25. Orleans, St. Bernard, Plaquemines, St. Charles, St. John the Baptist, St. James, Ascension, Assumption, Lafourche Interior, Iberville, Baton Rouge, Pointe Coupee, Concordia, Ouachita, Rapides, Avoyelles, Natchitoches, St. Landry and Attakapas; Or. Terr. A., 1807, I, sec. 9. Of these nineteen parishes only the name Attakapas has passed out of use. Although the name parish differs from that of county found in every other state, there is very little real difference. The parish is created by the state and as its agent administers state policy and has such authority as the state confers upon it. The increased demands of the residents of local areas for services similar to those of municipalities have resulted, through judicial and legislative interpretations, in making the parish (nominally a quasi-municipal corporation) closely resemble a municipality in its local governmental powers; cf. Carleton, op. cit., p. 82; Calhoun, loc. cit., pp. 90, 91.
26. Or. Terr. A., 1807, I, secs. 1, 2, 24.
27. Or. Terr. A., 1807, XVIII, secs. 1, 2; ibid., XXI, sec. 4.
28. Or. Terr. A., 1807, I, sec. 10.
29. Or. Terr. A., 1810, VIII.

the jury of "twelve inhabitants," heretofore appointed by the parish judge, was placed on an elective basis, while justices of the peace were denied a seat on the police jury.[30]

The powers of the parish judge were further reduced after the admission of the Territory of Orleans as a state. Parishes were for the first time divided into wards, and from each one police juror was elected. Justices of the peace were reinstated into the police jury, with the parish judge remaining as the presiding officer.[31] By 1824, however, the justices of the peace were removed from the police jury meetings, and in 1830, the parish judge also.[32] But in 1833 this latter officer was again made president of the police jury in St. Bernard, and certain other river parishes, and continued as such until his office was abolished in 1846.[33]

The re-organized police jury of 1813 was empowered to appoint a secretary, a parish treasurer, tax assessors, and constables.[34] The legislature likewise re-organized the court system. The supreme court was created. The superior court was abolished, and in its stead district courts were created with practically the same jurisdiction. The state was divided into judicial districts, and for each there was appointed a district judge and district attorney.[35] The parish, probate, and justices of the peace courts remained in about the same status as under the territorial government. The parish sheriff was made ex officio tax collector, and the offices of clerk of the district court and coroner were created in each parish.[36] Thus the only duties which remained to the parish judge were those of presiding officer of the parish and probate courts, president of the police jury, and recorder.

An effort was made to establish free public schools under the county system, but apparantly it was not until 1821 that parish schools were created in most of the parishes. These schools were placed in the hands of five trustees appointed by the police jury.[37]

The second State Constitution, adopted in 1845, made no provision for the parish and probate courts, therefore, the legislature divided the jurisdiction of these courts between the district court and the justices of the peace.[38] As a result, the office of parish judge was abolished and his extra function as recorder was vested in a separate officer.[39] This second constitution was, in certain respects, a much more liberal

---

30. Or. Terr. A., 1811, XXXVI.
31. La. A., 1813, p. 154, sec. 1.
32. La. A., 1824, p. 134, sec. 1; ibid., 1830, p. 130, sec. 3.
33. La. A., 1833, p. 91, sec. 2.
34. La. A., 1813, p. 154, sec. 5.
35. La. A., 1813, p. 18, secs. 4, 21.
36. La. A., 1813, p. 18, secs. 22, 23; ibid., 1814, p. 2,

sec. 1. The clerk was also clerk of the parish and probate courts, duties previously performed by the parish judge.
37. La. A., 1821, p. 62, sec. 1.
38. For the jurisdiction of the district court, see p. 70, and for justices of the peace, see p. 90.
39. La. A., 1846, #104, secs. 1, 2.

(Next entry, p. 44)

one than the first. It provided for the election of the clerk of court,
sheriff, coroner, and justices of the peace. Constables, who were not
mentioned in the constitution, were placed on an elective basis by the
legislature the following year. District judges continued as appointees
of the governor. The constitution, in addition, provided for the establishment of a free public school system throughout the state.

The Constitution of 1852 made no changes in parish government. It
did, however, provide for the election of district judges who, up to this
time, had been appointed by the governor. The Constitution of 1861 was
practically the same as that of 1852, except that under the later constitution, Louisiana became a confederate state. In 1864 a new constitution
was formed by a convention which met at New Orleans under the protection
of General Banks, commanding the Military Department of the Gulf. This
constitution was submitted to the popular vote and ratified, but the
state government organized under it was not recognized by Congress.[40]

After the Civil War another constitution (1868) was formed and a-
dopted. Under this constitution parish courts were re-established,[41]
and the office of supervisor of registration created.[42] A few parish
officers, such as tax assessor, board of school directors, and constables who had been elected since 1845 were made appointees of the governor.[43]

The post-reconstruction Constitution of 1879 abolished the parish
court created under the previous constitution;[44] merged the offices of
clerk of court and recorder, and created the court of appeal.[45] In 1871,
the legislature provided that police jury members be appointed by the
governor. They continued as gubernatorial appointees until 1896.[46]

The Constitution of 1898 restored normal government to the state,
and although since then two constitutions have been adopted, one in 1913,
and another in 1921, no major changes have been made by them. Since 1898
a few new offices have been created for the parishes. Some functions
which had been discarded have been restored, while others which had been
concentrated in the police jury have been assigned to other agencies.
The new offices created are, the parish board of health and the health

40. Thorpe, op. cit., III, p.
     1429.
41. Const., 1868, art. 69. The
     parish court was given con-
     current jurisdiction with
     the justices of the peace in
     cases up to $100, original
     jurisdiction in civil cases
     up to $500, complete probate
     jurisdiction, and minor
     criminal jurisdiction.
42. La. A., 1868, #56, sec. 2.
43. See Tax Assessor, Parish

     School Board, and Constables,
     pp. 104, 123, 100.
44. When the parish court was a-
     bolished its jurisdiction was
     transferred to the district
     court; cf. Const., 1879, art.
     80.
45. Const., 1879, arts. 95, 121.
46. La. A., 1871, #97, sec. 1;
     ibid., 1877, E. S., #57, sec.
     1; ibid., 1880, #37, sec. 1;
     ibid., 1894, #161, sec. 1.

unit,[47] the parish agricultural agent, and home demonstration agent.[48]
The registering of births and deaths, a function for which no obligatory
provision had been made since 1879, has been restored.[49] The board of
equalization (formerly the board of review) and the department of public
welfare discharge functions performed by the police jury before these
boards were created.[50]

Since 1914 there have been two optional forms of parish government
available in Louisiana. These are the police jury, in effect in all
parishes except Orleans, and the commission form which may be adopted by
a majority in a special election held for that purpose.[51]

The present set-up in St. Bernard parish is as follows: The administrative and legislative agency of the parish is in the police jury,
whose functions affect nearly every officer or body in the parish. The
records of this body include minutes of their meetings and ordinances.

The clerk of court is the recording officer in an ex officio capacity. He files, records, and indexes documents consisting chiefly of notarial and other original acts, such as conveyances, mortgages, donations,
liens, leases, powers of attorney, and other documents pertaining to real
and personal property and rights.

The judiciary is composed of the district court which has original
jurisdiction in civil, probate, and criminal matters, and appellate jurisdiction of cases from justices of the peace and municipal courts. Civil
and probate matters are appealable from the district court to the court
of appeal, while criminal cases are appealed directly to the supreme
court. The juvenile court, which is presided over by the district judge,
has jurisdiction in cases of juvenile delinquency and adoption of children under seventeen years of age. The jurisdiction of justices of the
peace extends in civil matters to suits involving less than $100, and in
criminal matters they act as committing magistrates only.

As clerk of the district and juvenile court, the clerk of court
keeps all the judicial records. These include a file of original civil,
probate, criminal and juvenile papers, docket books, minute books, and a
system of indexes. Coroner's inquests are filed and recorded by the
clerk of court, as well as petitions for naturalization. As a financial
officer of the court, the clerk keeps a record of funds belonging to minors, interdicts and persons unknown. In addition, he keeps a record of
marriage licenses, and records certificates and licenses issued to professional men and women.

Police and law enforcement powers are vested in the sheriff,

47. Const., 1898, art. 296; La.   50. La. A., 1920, #231; ibid.,
     A., 1918, #247, sec. 1; Ibid.,   1935, #14.
     1921, E. S., #79, sec. 11.   51. La. A., 1914, #190; Const.,
48. La. A., 1914, #8.   1921, art. XII, sec. 3.
49. La. A., 1918, #257.

constables, and district attorney. The police jury passes ordinances and regulations, the sheriff and his deputies enforce them and execute process of the district and juvenile courts. Constables serve process issued by the justices of the peace. The district attorney represents the state when prosecuting crimes committed in the parish.

The financial functions performed by parish officers and employees are tax administration, management of the financial affairs of the parish, and the trusteeship of funds held for individuals in court procedure. The principal financial agencies are the police jury, the board of equalization, tax assessor, sheriff and ex officio tax collector, and the parish treasurer. The police jury levies taxes, appropriates funds, and authorizes payments. The assessor lists property and its valuation; the board of equalization reviews the assessments; the sheriff as tax collector collects the taxes and deposits them with an authorized fiscal agent. The parish treasurer keeps records of the parish funds, and deposits such funds with the fiscal agency. He pays out money only on order of the police jury, a court, or other authorized officer.[52]

Elections are conducted under the supervision of a board composed of two appointees of the governor, and the registrar of voters. This board appoints commissioners and a clerk for each polling place, distributes the necessary supplies and makes the final compilation of the votes. Citizens who desire to vote must first be registered by the sheriff who issues poll certificates, after which they are registered by the registrar of voters.

The administration of public schools is vested in a school board which has power to merge school districts, determine the number of schools to be opened, the number of teachers to be employed, and to make rules and regulations not inconsistent with the law. The parish superintendent, elected by the board, is ex officio secretary of the board and treasurer of school funds. He exercises supervisory powers over schools, teachers, and other school employees, and makes the necessary reports to the parish and state boards of education.

Parish health work is administered by a board of five members appointed by the police jury, or by a health unit when created by mutual agreement with the state and parish boards of health.

Social service and welfare work was administered by the police jury until 1936, when the department of public welfare was created. This department, composed of a board of five members and a parish director, administers all forms of public assistance. The parish director is the executive officer and secretary of the board and, when appointed by a court of competent jurisdiction, may serve as a probation officer.[53]

The parish agricultural agent is a parish-state-federal officer,

---

52. La. A., 1855, #293, sec. 3;   2641-2643.
    Rev. Stat., 1870, secs.   53. La. A., 1936, #14, sec. 12.

who acts as agent of the parish, state, and federal farm programs to aid
farmers financially and maintain soil fertility. He also carries on educational work on farm problems, and is assisted in this field by the
home demonstration agent.

In Louisiana most and nearly all important records of the parish
will be found in the office of the clerk of court and ex officio recorder. The record system in this office is a simple one. Notarial acts of
all kinds (the original instruments of conveyance, mortgage, or transfer
of property or rights) are deposited with the ex officio recorder, and
usually given a file number. These are usually bound in volumes, though
sometimes they are filed loosely in file drawers. Various filing methods are used. Sometimes all acts are bound in strict chronological se-
quence regardless of the type of instrument. In other offices they are
segregated by types, and in still others the acts of each notary are
kept together. All these original notarial acts are recorded in some
book in the office, e. g., conveyances are copied into the conveyance
record, conventional mortgages in the mortgage record, chattel mortgages
in the chattel mortgage record, and bonds in the bond book. Some instruments are recorded in two records, e. g., bonds are also recorded in
the mortgage record, and conveyances with mortgage are copied in both
the mortgage and conveyance records. Indexes to these records are var-
ied in nature. The usual practice in the past has been to make separate
indexes for each volume of a series, though in most of the larger parishes general indexes are available. Indexing projects under the sponsorship of the Works Progress Administration have been set up in most parishes and are preparing modern and complete direct and reverse indexes
to all of the principal records in the office of the clerk and ex officio recorder.

The judicial records are kept by the clerk of court in a somewhat
similar manner. When a suit or case is instituted it is entered in the
appropriate docket book and given a docket number. All the original
papers relating to the suit or case are placed together as they are
filed, usually in a folder labeled with the title and docket number.
The documents filed are entered in the docket book with the filing date,
and often the filing fee charged. The proceedings of the suit or case
are entered in the minute book, and after the conclusion of court procedure all of the documents and the court orders and judgments are recorded in a judicial record book. Various types of indexes to the court
records are kept, the more usual type being that which gives the docket
number by which all of the records of the case or suit can be located.

Thus it will be seen that parish records most consulted by the public are available in the office of the clerk of court and ex officio recorder.

The administrative records of the parish will be found in the police jury minutes, though in some parishes compilations of ordinances
are made. The principal financial records are kept by the parish treasurer, who is an appointee of the police jury. His books are audited by
the state auditor.

The records of most other parishes officers are uniform throughout the state. All records which relate to the assessment and collection of taxes, for example, are kept on printed forms furnished the parish officers by the state.

3. HOUSING, CARE, AND ACCESSIBILITY OF THE RECORDS

The first courthouse of St. Bernard Parish was located in the village of Violet, where the present St. Bernard Church now stands. It was afterward removed to the post office site,[1] where it remained until the present site in St. Bernard village was donated by Vincent Nunez. This grant was made on March 7, 1848, and consisted of a lot of ground situated about three miles from the Mississippi on the left bank of Bayou Terre aux Boeufs.[2] A courthouse was apparently built on this plot of ground soon afterward.

Some twenty years later, a grand jury report declared that "we find that the Court House is totally unfit for the purpose for which it was created, and is now and has been for a long time past in a dangerous condition and that in order to prevent accident and save human life and perhaps the parish against heavy damages we earnestly recommend that the same be forthwith raized ¡sic¡ and a new one built by the parish."[3] No immediate action seems to have resulted, though an act of 1874 authorized the governor to appoint three citizens of the parish as commissioners "to select a suitable location not more than a half mile from the Mississippi river and the Mexican Gulf Ship Canal." In 1875 the commissioners were ordered to secure a lot for the parish not to exceed five acres and not to cost more than $1,000, and build a courthouse and jail not to exceed $15,000.[4]

Even this act of the legislature appears to have been ineffective for, in the following year, we are told, that the grand jury had "repeatedly pronounced on the unsafeness of the present courthouse" and that "the District Judge has refused to hold court in the courthouse owing to its dilapidated condition." The police jury thereupon resolved that "the President of the Police Jury . . . empowered and directed to lease a suitable building temporarily for the use of the Parish as a Court House."[5] Accordingly, a building known as the Mississippi Club House, which was situated on the Mississippi river, was leased for one year at a rental of $900.[6] The necessary alterations were made at a cost of $700.[7]

The next year this building was purchased by the parish for $3,500 and the land on which it stood was donated to the parish by the Crescent City Live Stock Landing and Slaughter House Company. It was described as a "large one story frame building raised on brick pillars" located on Levee, or Peters, Street.[8]

Seemingly this action did not meet with the approval of the state legislature for, in 1877, an act directed the local authorities of St.

1. Goodspeed, op. cit., p. 197.
2. See entry 2, "Notarial Acts,"
    Livre Second, folder A., p.
    162.
3. See entry 1, "Minutes of the
    Police Jury," Apr. 1, 1872,
    p. 76.
4. La. A., 1874, #130, sec. 2.

5. See entry 1, "Minutes of the
    Police Jury," May 3, 1875,
    p. 161.
6. Ibid., May 10, 1875, p. 167.
7. Ibid., May 13, 1875, pp. 175,
    176.
8. Ibid., May 2, 1876, pp.
    267-269.

Bernard Parish to "remove back to the legal courthouse of said parish" and also repealed the act of 1874.[9] A police jury committee, in consequence, examined the old building on Bayou Terre aux Boeufs and reported that it was their opinion "that a new building need be erected."[10] A resolution was therefore adopted "to have an election by the people to authorize removal of the courthouse to be held on the 2nd Monday in December 1877, and to determine whether the seat of Justice remain on the Bayou Terre aux Boeufs or on the Mississippi."[11] This was done by virtue of permission granted by the legislature.[12]

We do not know the results of this action since the police jury minutes are missing between December 4, 1877 and April 24, 1880. It would appear, however, that nothing was accomplished for, in 1880, the police jury resolved "that all monies derived from the collection of licenses" be set aside for repairing the courthouse and jail. A committee was appointed to receive bids for repairs, and the tax collector was instructed to turn over all sums derived from licenses to the parish treasurer, who set this money aside to defray these expenses. The committee came to the conclusion that the jail could be repaired, but that the courthouse would have to be rebuilt. Plans and specifications for such repairs and rebuilding were ordered from N. A. Freret, architect, who was paid $50. The only bid, that of L. N. Olivier, was accepted. He agreed to repair the jail and rebuild the courthouse for $2,325.[13]

This building was destroyed by fire on March 2, 1884, and with it most of the records prior to 1877. Some few records of the parish judges were saved.[14]

The seat of justice was returned temporarily to the former location in the old Mississippi Club building, but after a short interval removed to a building on Bayou Terre aux Boeufs which was leased for an indefinit period from C. D. Armstrong at a monthly rental of twenty dollars.[15]

Some four years later a committee was appointed by the police jury to examine the building known as the Shell Beach Fishing and Gun Club wit a view to demolishing it and using the material to build a courthouse on the old site.[16]

This plan, however, did not prove feasible and bids were asked for the erection of a new courthouse. That of H. L. Turner was accepted.

9. La. A., 1877, #34, sec. 1.
10. See entry 1, "Minutes of the
    Police Jury," June 4, 1877,
    p. 334.
11. Ibid., Nov. 3, 1877, p. 363;
    Afterward this resolution
    was suspended until 1878; cf.
    ibid., Dec. 3, 1877, p. 365.
12. La. A., 1877, #34, secs. 3,
    4, 5.
13. See entry 1, "Minutes of the
    Police Jury," Apr. 24, 1880,
    p. 24; May 3, 1880, p. 26;
    June 7, 1880, p. 33.
14. See entries 2, 3, 4, 5.
15. See entry 1, "Minutes of the
    Police Jury," Mar. 17, 1884,
    p. 178.
16. Ibid., March 12, 1888, p.
    324.

He agreed to build it for $4000, and to finish by December 31, 1888.[17]
He, however, was granted an extension of time.[18] The building was finally accepted on August 19, 1889, and a contract made to remove documents and furniture to the new courthouse by August 24.[19]

On January 20, 1914 a special election was held for the purpose of
obtaining a vote on the proposition to authorize the police jury to
erect a new courthouse. The vote was affirmative, and the police jury
proposed the issuance of bonds for the sum of $100,000 to pay the build-
ing expenses.[20] The amount was afterward reduced to $85,000.[21] Bids
were then asked and the Jefferson Construction Company was awarded the
contract on its bid of $64,893.[22] Work was begun immediately and on May
4, 1915 the building was accepted by the police jury.[23] This building,
situated in the village of St. Bernard on the Bayou Terre aux Boeufs, is
now in use, though the recent legislature has granted permission to submit to the voters of the parish a proposition for removal of the courthouse to another site.[24]

The present courthouse, a modern three story red brick structure,
has adequate office space for the present needs of the parish. The first
floor is occupied by the offices of the clerk of court, the sheriff, and
the tax assessor, and has rooms for the use of the home demonstration
agent and the police jury. On the second floor is the courtroom, and
offices of the department of public welfare.[25] None of these offices is
crowded and there is ample storage space for non-current records. There
are few accommodations for the use of persons wishing to consult records
except in the clerk's office, where a large table and several chairs are
provided. The lighting and ventilation are uniformly good throughout
the building. The walls and ceilings are plastered, and the floors of
offices are of wood, while those of the halls and the stairways are of
concrete. The building is considered to be approximately 75 percent
fireproof.

The police jury room in the courthouse is used only for meetings of
that body. The minute books, with the exception of two of the early volumes which are in the vault of the clerk of court are kept at the home
of the police jury secretary in St. Bernard village. The financial records of the police jury are kept at the home of the parish treasurer in
Violet.

The office of the clerk of court and ex officio recorder contains a

17. Ibid., Apr. 9, 1888, p. 326.
18. Ibid., Dec. 3, 1888, p. 334.
19. Ibid., Aug. 19, 1888, p. 355.
20. Ibid., 1895-1914, pp. 530,
    537, 556, 558.
21. Ibid., Apr. 4, 1914, p. 572.
22. See entry 47, "Mortgage
    Record," vol. 19, p. 273.
23. See cancelation of bond and
    contract in "Mortgage Rec-
    ord," vol. 19, p. 420.
24. La. A., 1938, #65. The vot-
    ers approved this and work
    has been begun on a new
    building in the village of
    Chalmette.
25. See floor plans, pp. 32-34.

Housing, Care, and Accessibility
   of the Records

fireproof vault in which all his records are kept. As has been stated
above, many of the parish records were destroyed in the courthouse fire
of March 2, 1884. The important records which were saved include the
notarial acts of the commandant, and of the parish judges. These are in
very poor condition and should be copied to preserve them. Workers of
the Historical Records Survey re-assembled the scattered pages in proper
order and placed them in folders in the vault in the office of clerk of
court and recorder. Though seldom consulted they are an important source
of information on the early history of the parish. Bound records are located on steel roller shelves and unbound material is contained in steel
filing cabinets. Material contained in some of the older records is difficult to locate because indexes to these records are lacking. Another
cause of confusion is the practice followed in the past of entering records of a totally dissimilar character in parts of the same volume. The
current records, however, are properly segregated, and are well kept.
The records in this office are open to the public during office hours.

   The district attorney had an office on the second floor of the courthouse, but kept no records there. This office is at present being used by
the welfare department.

   The office of the sheriff and ex officio tax collector contains few
records. The current ones are kept in a safe in the office, while older
records are stored on wooden shelves behind sliding panels.

   The tax assessor keeps only current records in his office. These
are located under a wooden counter, which provides sufficient space for
those who wish to consult them. Older records are destroyed.

   The registrar of voters has no office, but during registration
periods uses the office of the clerk of court, and keeps his records in
the vault.

   The parish school board had two offices in the building, but these
are used at present by the home demonstration agent, and the commodity
distribution. All of the current records will be found in the office of
the parish superintendent in the Joseph Maumus High School in Arabi.

   The department of public welfare occupies two rooms on the second
floor, and its records, which are confidential, are kept in steel file
cabinets.

   The parish agent has his office in Arabi, but keeps no records
there. The records of extension and club work are kept in the office of
the home demonstration agent at the courthouse. The Federal programs
records are kept in the office of the farm agent at the Plaquemines
Parish courthouse in Pointe a la Hache.

   The home demonstration agent has office space in the courthouse
where here records and those of the parish agent relative to agricultural
extension and club work are kept.

(First entry, p. 44)

4. LIST OF ABBREVIATIONS, SYMBOLS, AND EXPLANATORY NOTES

A.	Act, Acts
alph.	alphabetical, alphabetically
approx.	approximate, approximately
arr.	arranged, arrangement
art.	article
aver.	average
C. C.	Civil Code
C. C. C.	Civilian Conservation Corps
C. C. P.	Code of Civil Procedure
C. Cr. P.	Code of Criminal Procedure (1928)
cf.	compare
chap.	chapter
comp.	compiler
Const.	Constitution
C. P.	Code of Practice
C. W. A.	Civil Works Administration
dept.	department
ed.	editor
e. g.	for example
E. S.	Extra Session
et al.	and others
ff.	following pages
ft.	foot, feet (see symbols)
hdw.	handwritten
ibid.	the same reference
i. e.	that is
in.	inch, inches (see symbols)
incl.	inclusive
I. P. A. La.	Inventory of Parish Archives of Louisiana
La.	Louisiana
La. A.	Acts of the Louisiana State Legislatures
La. Hist. Q.	Louisiana Historical Quarterly
loc. cit.	the place cited
N. Y. A.	National Youth Administration
no., nos.	number, numbers
numer.	numerical, numerically
op. cit.	work cited
Or. Terr. A.	Acts of Orleans Territorial Council & Legislatures
p., pp.	page, pages
Rev. Stat.	Revised Statutes
sec.	section, sections
sic.	thus, according to copy
So.	Southern
St.	street
trans.	translator
U. S.	United States
vol., vols.	volume, volumes
W. P. A.	Works Progress Administration
--	current
'	foot, feet (see ft.)

If no statement is made concerning the condition of a record, it is assumed that it is in good condition.

Volume, file box, and map dimensions are given in inches.

Exact titles of records are in capitals, assigned titles in capitals, but enclosed in brackets. An assigned title added in brackets beside an exact title to explain or correct the exact title is given in initial capitals only. Two dashes after a date indicate that the record is current.

Records, unless otherwise indicated, are located in the parish courthouse and in the office under which they are listed.

Citations to the acts of the Orleans Territorial or Louisiana Legislature refer to the number and section of the act, except for the early acts. The Orleans Territorial Acts are cited by the chapter numbers in roman numerals, while acts of the years 1813-27, and 1830-36 are cited by the page numbers of the beginning of the act in the official publication.

The cross references placed under subject headings refer to records which may be classified under a different department of the same office or in another office, but which deal with the same subject. For example, the probate records properly belong to different courts. These are entered under the proper court with subject heading cross references, see entries 73, 83.

The title line cross reference is intended to show that the record completes a series, and is complemented by a body-of-entry references. The entry containing the title line reference is usually an artificial entry designed to give prominence to records which though differing in character are kept or recorded together. We also use this style of cross reference to show different types of records which, though totally dissimilar, happened to have been recorded in the same book, see entries 70, 74.

Where entries are closely related as, for example, an original notarial act and its true copy, the third paragraph cross reference is used. These references are intended to illustrate the records system of the office and the relation between records of different offices.

See pages 18 and 19 for a description of the records system in St. Bernard Parish.

(First entry, p. 44)

I. POLICE JURY

The development of the administrative and governing body of St. Bernard Parish has its basis in earlier French and Spanish forms of local government. Under these regimes the commandant of the district was the principal figure in the administration of regional affairs. He was assisted by syndics who acted as his subordinates over smaller areas.[1]

After the purchase of Louisiana by the United States, the Territory of Orleans was divided into twelve counties, for each of which a county judge and justices of the peace were appointed. These new officers were vested with all the powers previously exercised by the commandant and syndics.[2] In 1807, the twelve counties were replaced, insofar as local government was concerned, by nineteen civil parishes, of which St. Bernard was one. Under this system, the administrative functions were placed in the hands of the parish judge, justices of the peace, and a jury of twelve inhabitants acting as a body.[3] This body was spoken of in the beginning as a "jury", "parish assembly", or "parish jury", but in 1811 it was for the first time referred to in a law by its present name "police jury".[4]

In the same year (1811) the "jury of twelve inhabitants", who had hitherto been appointed by the parish judge, were ordered to be elected by the inhabitants for a term of two years. At the same time justices of the peace were removed from police jury membership.[5] Two years later St. Bernard, with the other parishes of the state, was divided into wards, from each of which one representative was elected to the police jury for a term of two years. The members elected at the first election were to be divided by lot into two classes, those of the first class holding office for two years, those of the second for one year only, so that the police jury was renewed every year by one-half. Justices of the peace were again allowed to take their seats as members.[6]

In 1816 the parish judge and justices of the peace were authorized to divide their parish into not more than twelve nor less than five wards. From each ward one representative was to be elected to the police jury for a term of two years. This law did not mention justices of the peace as members of the police jury.[7] Hence, a year later, justices of the peace were authorized to take their seats as members, but no certain number of them was necessary to do business in any case whatever.[8] They continued as members until 1824, when a law provided that "no justice of the peace shall, by virtue of his office have a seat as member of the

1. Carleton, op. cit., pp. 17, 19, 26.
2. Or. Terr. A., 1805, XLIV, sec. 1; ibid., XXV, secs. 1, 2.
3. From this body developed the present police jury. It has never been established or organized by constitution, but only by acts of the legislature.

4. Or. Terr. A., 1807, XVIII, sec. 1; ibid., 1810, XII; ibid., XXII; ibid., 1811, VII; ibid., XXXVI, sec. 3.
5. Or. Terr. A., 1811, XXXVI, sec. 3.
6. La. A., 1813, p. 154.
7. La. A., 1816, p. 160.
8. La. A., 1817, p. 154.

police jury."[9]

    Police jurymen were elected, one from each ward, until 1854, in St. Bernard Parish.[10] In this year a special act of the legislature divided St. Bernard into six police jury wards, from each of which two members were to be elected to the police jury.[11] In 1871, the number of police jurors was reduced to five for each parish. These were appointed by the governor until the election of 1872, at which time they were to be elected, and every two years thereafter. No two of the members could be appointed or elected from the same ward.[12] This law was repealed in 1877 and it was provided that the governor appoint, by and with the advice of the senate, in such country parishes as he saw fit, additional police jurors not exceeding five. These, with the jurors elected at the last general election, were to constitute the police jury of each parish until the next general election.[13]

    The term of office of all police jurors in the state was terminated on the first Monday of April 1880, and the governor was authorized, by and with the advice of the senate, to appoint their successors until the next general election.[14] In 1882, however, the governor was again authorized to appoint successors to those appointed in 1880. These in turn were to hold office until the general election in 1888.[15] In 1884 the governor was authorized to appoint one additional police juror for each ward that contained 5,000 inhabitants or part thereof in excess of 2,500.[16]

    Two years later another law was passed making it the duty of the governor to appoint police jurors to succeed those whose term would expire in 1888. These appointees were to hold office until the general election of 1892.[17] This method of selecting police jurors continued until 1896, when the office was again placed on an elective basis. One member was to be elected from each ward for a term of four years.[18] In 1908 provisions were made for additional police jurors in parishes having less than 50,000 population. This law, which is in effect today, is the same as Act 94 of 1884, except that such additional jurors are elected.[19] In St. Bernard Parish there are seven police jurors representing the seven wards of the parish.[20]

    The qualifications necessary for police jury membership prescribed in 1811 were: to be a respectable citizen and owner of a freehold in the

9. La. A., 1824, p. 134, sec. I.

10. La. A., 1816, p. 160.

11. La. A., 1854, #235, secs. 1, 2.

12. La. A., 1871, #97, sec. 3.

13. La. A., 1877, E. S., #57, secs. 1, 2, 5.

14. La. A., 1880, #37, sec. 1.

15. La. A., 1882, #94, sec. 1.

16. La. A., 1884, #94, sec. 1.

17. La. A., 1886, #20, sec. 1.

18. La. A., 1890, #119, sec. 1; Ibid., 1894, #161.

19. La. A., 1908, #279.

20. State of Louisiana Roster of Officials, Corrected to January 15, 1937, compiled by E. A. Conway, Secretary of State, p. 95.

parish.[21] In 1829 the candidate for this office had to have the same
qualifications as were required for members of the lower house of the
state legislature. These were United States citizenship, residence in
the state for two years, and in the parish for one year prior to his
election, and ownership of landed property to the value of $500.[22] In
1850 candidates for the office of police juror in St. Bernard Parish
were required also to have been residents of the ward for three months
previous to election.[23] Since 1894 a candidate to the office must possess the qualifications cited above, except that he shall own in his own
right, or whose wife shall own in her own right, property of an assessed
value of at least $250 in the parish, and in addition be able to read
and write.[24]

Until police jurors were made elective in 1811, vacancies were
filled by appointment by the parish judge. In that year vacancies of
three members or more were filled by an election called by the parish
judge.[25] Two years later when parishes were divided into wards, vacancies occurring in any ward were filled by a special election called in
that ward.[26] In 1847 it was made the duty of the president of the police jury to order elections to fill vacancies in the police jury.[27]
Since 1916, the governor has been empowered to fill vacancies occurring
in any parish office until the next general election.[28]

The presiding officer or president of the parish meeting was, until
1813, the parish judge, or in his absence one of the members of the jury
elected by ballot.[29] In this year a law provided that in case the parish
judge was absent one of the justices of the peace, elected by ballot,
should preside at the police jury meeting.[30] In 1816 the parish judge
lost his right to vote, but could deliberate with the police jury on all
subjects that came within its jurisdiction. In his absence the members
were authorized to choose one from among themselves to act as president.[31]
Two years later a supplementary act provided that one of the justices of
the peace of the parish be designated as senior justice, who, in the absence of the parish judge, was authorized to preside at police jury meetings.[32] When the justices of the peace were finally removed from the
police jury in 1824, that body was empowered to appoint, in the absence
of the parish judge, a president pro tempore from among themselves.[33]
The parish judge continued to act as president of the police jury until

---

21. Or. Terr. A., 1811, XXXVI,
    sec. 3.
22. La. A., 1829, #23; cf. Const.,
    1812, art. II, sec. 4.
23. La. A., 1850, #346, sec. 2.
24. La. A., 1894, #94.
25. Or. Terr. A., 1811, XXXVI,
    sec. 3.
26. La. A., 1813, p. 154, sec.
    3; ibid., 1816, p. 160,
    sec. 8.
27. La. A., 1847, #106, sec. 2;
    Rev. Stat., 1870, sec. 2737;

La. A., 1871, #97, sec. 4;
ibid., 1877, E. S., #57,
sec. 4; ibid., 1894, #161.
28. La. A., 1916, #236.
29. Or. Terr. A., 1811, XXXVI,
    sec. 3.
30. La. A., 1813, p. 154, sec.
    4.
31. La. A., 1816, p. 160, sec.
    2.
32. La. A., 1818, p. 72, sec. 6.
33. La. A., 1824, p. 134, sec.
    2.

1830, when that body was authorized to appoint annually a president from their own membership.[34] The effect of this act, however, was suspended for certain parishes, among which was St. Bernard, by an act of 1833, which restored the presidency of the police jury to the parish judge.[35] He acted in this capacity until 1847, even though his office had been abolished by the Constitution of 1845. Since then the president of the police jury has been appointed by the police jury from among its own members.[36] Since 1850 the clerk of the district court has been authorized to convene the police jury whenever there was a vacancy in the office of the president.[37]

In the beginning, the police jury required a quorum of nine members to pass regulations or to do business.[38] In 1813 this was changed so that it was necessary to have only a majority of the members, together with one-third of the justices of the peace, to deliberate and act, except in cases when tax levies were discussed. To impose such levies it was necessary that two-thirds of the members be present, exclusive of the judge and justices of the peace.[39] Today a quorum is required to pass ordinances and a two-thirds vote to re-district the parish into wards.[40]

Soon after the establishment of the police jury, it was given authority to appoint many of the minor parish officials. These included a parish treasurer, a clerk of the police jury, constables,[41] tax assessors,[42] syndics, or inspectors of roads and levees,[43] and school administrators.[44] Of these officers the clerk, or secretary, of the police jury, the parish treasurer, and road and levee overseers are appointees of the police jury today. In recent years the police jury has been authorized to combine the offices of parish treasurer and secretary of the police jury.[45] This, however, has not been done in St. Bernard Parish.

The first duties delegated to the parish assembly, or police jury, were to deliberate upon and make regulations relative to roads, bridges, and levees, local administration, and equal distribution of taxes.[46] From this beginning the public works powers of the police jury have been

34. La. A., 1830, p. 130, sec. 3.
35. La. A., 1833, p. 91, sec. 1; ibid., 1839, #44, sec. 10.
36. La. A., 1847, #106, sec. 3; Rev. Stat., 1870, sec. 2735; La. A., 1871, #97, sec. 2.
37. La. A., 1850, #37; Rev. Stat., 1870, sec. 2733.
38. Or. Terr. A., 1811, XXXVI, sec. 3.
39. La. A., 1813, p. 154, sec. 4; ibid., 1816, p. 160, sec. 2.
40. Opinions and Reports of the Attorney General of the

State of Louisiana from April 1, 1934, to April 1, 1936, pp. 844, 845.
41. La. A., 1813, p. 154, sec. 5.
42. La. A., 1813, p. 218, sec. 4; ibid., 1814, p. 48, sec. 7.
43. La. A., 1820, p. 52, sec. 1; ibid., 1898, #115.
44. La. A., 1821, p, 62, sec. 1; see Parish School Board, p. 123
45. La. A., 1924, #122, sec. 1.
46. Or. Terr. A., 1807, XVIII, sec. 1; La. A., 1831, p. 4, secs. 1, 2.

expanded to include in addition supervision of the construction, repair, and maintenance of streams, ferries, navigable river,[47] navigation canals,[48] rice flumes in levees,[49] sewerage,[50] and gravity drainage systems.[51] Recent laws have empowered the police jury to own and operate gas plants,[52] parish fair grounds,[53] recreational systems,[54] and airports.[55] One restriction on its public works power is the requirement to advertise for bids before letting out contracts.[56]

Power to levy taxes was granted, under the county system, to the county judge and justices of the peace. This levy was limited to assessments of real and personal property for the purpose of erecting, or procuring a suitable courthouse, and for other expenses which were chargable by law to the county.[57] When the parish police jury was formed these powers were conferred upon that body, and additional authority to levy taxes for the upkeep and repair of levees,[58] public works,[59] and for public schools.[60] A law of 1830 permitted the police jury of St. Bernard to levy a license tax on grog-shops and in 1852 on drinking houses, on the sale of intoxicating liquors, as well as a tax for the support of the "poor and necessitous".[61]

Since Reconstruction the police jury has been allowed to impose many special taxes. These embrace special levies for roads,[62] for any work of public improvement,[63] and for drainage districts.[64] License taxes, in addition to those levied by the state, may be collected from all persons or firms doing business in the parish.[65] Since the repeal of the eighteenth amendment, parish licenses may be imposed on the sale of wines, beer, ale, porter, and other liquors.[66] The police jury was

47. La. A., 1813, p. 154, sec. 5; ibid., 1898, #115.
48. La. A., 1921, E. S., #42.
49. La. A., 1884, #84; ibid., 1921, E. S., #100, sec. 1.
50. La. A., 1924, #222, sec. 1.
51. La. A., 1924, #208, sec. 1.
52. La. A., 1920, #21; ibid., 1921, E. S., #70.
53. La. A., 1921, E. S., #112.
54. La. A., 1924, #200.
55. La. A., 1928, #24, #239; ibid., 1928, E. S., #5; ibid., 1930, E. S., #13; ibid., 1936, #222.
56. La. A., 1935, 4th E. S., #20.
57. Or. Terr. A., 1805, XLIII, sec. 1.
58. Or. Terr. A., 1810, XI.
59. La. A., 1813, p. 154, sec. 5.
60. La. A., 1821, p. 63, sec. 4; ibid., 1847, #225; ibid., 1898, #131.
61. La. A., 1830, p. 130, sec. 5;

ibid., 1852, #105, #238; ibid., 1855, #126; Rev. Stat., 1870, sec. 2743.
62. La. A., 1867, #197; Const., 1898, art. 291.
63. La. A., 1880, #84; ibid., 1886, #35; ibid., 1894, #153.
64. La. A., 1888, #107; ibid., 1890, #83, #142; ibid., 1894, #37; ibid., 1896, #125; ibid., 1900, #12, #114.
65. La. A., 1924, #205; ibid., 1926, #299; ibid., 1928, #241; ibid., 1932, #111, #112, #138, #190; ibid., 1934, #88; ibid., 1934, 1st E. S., #16; ibid., 1935, 3rd E. S., #2; ibid., 1936, #18, #291.
66. La. A., 1933, E. S., #2; ibid., 1934, #15; ibid., 1934, 3rd E. S., #1; ibid., 1935, 1st E. S., #3; ibid., 2nd E. S., #24.

allowed to levy a tax on gasoline and other motor fuel sold in the parish, not to exceed one cent per gallon in any one year,[67] but since 1934 the proceeds of this tax must be deposited with the state treasurer for use of the Emergency Relief Administration (now department of public welfare).[68] Certain special taxes must be endorsed by a majority of the voters and property taxpayers at an election before being imposed.[69]

Toward the end of Reconstruction a limitation was placed upon parochial expenditures by forbidding parish officers to issue warrants, and the police jury was given authority to contract with parish officers for a fixed compensation in place of fees and charges previously allowed by law.[70] Police jurors cannot draw money from the parish treasury other than their per diem and mileage, be interested in parish contracts, or deal in parish paper.[71]

The police jury is empowered to issue public improvement bonds when authorized to do so by a vote of a majority, in number and amount, of the taxpayers. Such bonds may be issued for the construction and maintenance of public roads, highways and bridges, courthouses, jails, hospitals, and other public buildings, for drainage canals, dikes and levees, as well as for equipment and furnishings for such works.[72] The avails of the "general alimony tax" (real property tax) may also be funded into negotiable bonds.[73] The police jury is permitted to borrow money from any governmental agency of the United States.[74] Such loans, including money obtained from the sale of bonds, cannot be expended except under the supervision, and with the approval, of the state advisory board.[75]

The police jury served as a board of review of assessments from 1882 until 1920, when a separate board, known as the board of equalization, was created. It met annually in this capacity to examine the assessments and to determine if the valuations were equitable.[76]

As early as 1817 the police jury was given the power to sue any

67. La. A., 1928, E. S., #15.
68. La. A., 1934, 1st. E. S., #21; ibid., 1936, #17; cf. Opinions and Reports of the Attorney General from April 1, 1934, to April 1, 1936, pp. 843, 844.
69. Const., 1879, art. 209; La. A., 1882, #41, #126; Const., 1898, art. 232; La. A., 1898, #131; ibid., 1910, #270.
70. La. A., 1877, E. S., #30.
71. La. A., 1898, #22.
72. La. A., 1899, E. S., #5; ibid., 1900, #114; ibid., 1906, #95, #186; ibid., 1910,

#197, #256; ibid., 1912, #132, #141; Const., 1913, art. 281; La. A., 1917, E. S., #30; ibid., 1924, #11, #171, #218; ibid., 1932, #130, #236.
73. La. A., 1922, #40.
74. La. A., 1934, #222.
75. La. A., 1935, 2nd E. S., #10.
76. La. A., 1882, #96, sec. 23; ibid., 1886, #98; ibid., 1888, #85; ibid., 1898, #170; ibid., 1916, #140, sec. 15; ibid., 1918, #211, sec. 4, see p. 111.

person for whose account it had made repairs on roads, levees, and bridges.[77] This law, as interpreted by the supreme court, "necessarily implied" that the police jury could be sued as "incidental to express powers granted".[78]

The police jury was granted the privilege of electing one beneficiary cadet to the Louisiana State University and Agricultural and Mechanical College, and could appropriate a sum, not in excess of $250 per annum, for the expense of such cadet.[79] A like sum could also be appropriated to defray the expenses of female students attending the Louisiana Industrial Institute, the Southwestern Industrial Institute, or the State Normal College.[80]

Provision for the needs of the "poor and necessitous" was inaugurated by law in 1852.[81] In 1880 this was made mandatory on the parish, except for the poor residing within municipal corporations.[82] Since the turn of the century, other laws have been passed enlarging the social service activities of the parish. These include the burial of paupers at parish expense, the appropriation of a limited sum annually for the support of charity hospitals, or similar institutions,[83] the authority to contract with charitable societies for the care and support of children,[84] the contribution of limited sums for the needy blind,[85] for mothers having dependent children,[86] for the treatment of tuberculosis,[87] for needy war veterans and their beneficiaries,[88] for needy students,[89] and for crippled persons over fifty years of age.[90] The recent creation of the state and parish boards of public welfare has resulted in the concentration of all forms of parish social service and welfare activities under their supervision.[91]

Police powers of legislative and administrative nature were granted to the police jury at an early date. Modified and supplemented at various times, these powers have included the authority to make and enforce regulations for the preservation of public safety,[92] for regulating taverns and the sale of liquor,[93] the form and height of

77. La. A., 1817, p. 154, sec. 3; ibid., 1828, #71; ibid., 1898, #115; ibid., 1902, #202.
78. Calhoun, loc. cit., p. 128.
79. La. A., 1886, #100.
80. La. A., 1902, #158.
81. La. A., 1852, #238; ibid., 1898, #115, #202.
82. La. A., 1880, #42; cf. Const., 1879, art. 163.
83. La. A., 1912, #181; ibid., 1926, #211.
84. La. A., 1926, #182.
85. La. A., 1928, #101, sec. 6; ibid., 1936, #53, sec. 2.
86. La. A., 1920, #209; ibid.,

1928, #228; ibid., 1930, #46.
87. La. A., 1930, #60.
88. La. A., 1932, #182.
89. La. A., 1932, #196.
90. La. A., 1932, #52.
91. La. A., 1936, #14; see Parish Department of Public Welfare, p. 132.
92. Or. Terr. A., 1810, XII.
93. La. A., 1813, p. 154, sec. 5; ibid., 1852, #105; ibid., 1855, #126; Rev. Stat., 1870, sec. 2743; La. A., 1878, #84; ibid., 1898, #115; ibid., 1902, #202; ibid., 1928, #234.

fences,[94] the punishment of trespass,[95] the regulation of hawkers and peddlers,[96] the punishment of vagrancy,[97] the authority to work and hire out parish prisoners,[98] to prohibit gambling with cards,[99] and the regulation of traffic on public highways within the parish.[100]

The authority to enact measures to regulate cattle, sheep, horses, and mules has been granted to the police jury.[101] It has been authorized to constitute itself a board of livestock sanitary commissioners, to enact and enforce ordinances for suppressing contagious diseases affecting livestock, and for tick eradication.[102] They may also enact measures for the prevention of cruelty to animals,[103] and for the preservation of wild game and fish.[104]

Records of the police jury include minutes of the proceedings of the meetings, miscellaneous administrative records, and compiled ordinances. Reports of various officers and committees will usually be found in the minute books. The financial records of the police jury will be found under the parish treasurer, who is an appointee of this body. Since 1882, the police jury has had authority to make and renew indexes and re-copy parish records when necessary.[105]

In St. Bernard Parish the custodian of police jury records is the secretary. Like the treasurer, he is an employee and not a member of the police jury.

Proceedings

1. MINUTES OF THE POLICE JURY, Mar. 29, 1870-Dec. 3, 1877; Apr. 14, 1880--. 6 vols. Missing: 1807-Feb. 1870.
Record of proceedings of the regular and special meetings of the police jury, including resolutions, motions, ordinances, annual budgets, reports of parish officers and committees, giving date and place of meeting, names of members in attendance, names of members absent, and

---

94. Or. Terr. A., 1807, XVIII, sec. 2; La. A., 1813, p. 154, sec. 5; ibid., 1880, #55; ibid., 1898, #115; ibid., 1902, #202.
95. La. A., 1825, p. 62; ibid., 1898, #115, ibid., 1902, #202.
96. La. A., 1900, #128; ibid., 1932, #190; ibid., 1934, #88.
97. La. A., 1904, #178; ibid., 1908, #205.
98. La. A., 1894, #29; ibid., 1902, #46; ibid., 1904, #191.
99. La. A., 1918, #183.
100. La. A., 1926, #232.
101. Or. Terr. A., 1807, XVIII, sec. 2; La. A., 1813, p. 154, sec. 5; ibid., 1824, p. 62, sec. 3; ibid., 1886, #111; ibid., 1898, #115; ibid., 1902, #202.
102. La. A., 1894, #147; ibid., 1917, E. S., #25; ibid., 1920, #254.
103. La. A., 1888, #19.
104. La. A., 1896, #60; ibid., 1908, #207; ibid., 1912, #239; ibid., 1914, #135; ibid., 1926, #259, secs. 1, 2. The latter act authorized the police jury to appoint game and fish commissioners.
105. La. A., 1882, #90.

offices affecting the lands of the parish,50 maps of municipalities,51 lists of property purchased for the state,52 plats of subdivisions,53 laborers' liens and privileges,54 and lists of delinquent taxpayers.55

The records of the clerk of court as ex officio recorder in St. Bernard Parish are kept together with the court records. They are for the most part bound in large volumes, are open to the inspection of the public during office hours, and will be transferred to his successor in office.

Notaries Public*

From the period of exploration and discovery, the notary public has been important in the economic and political life of Louisiana. La Salle, when he took possession of Louisiana for France, confirmed this action by means of a notarial act dated April 9, 1682.56

By an ordinance of August 2, 1717, the basic law under which notaries were to operate was promulgated. In the preamble, the ordinance states that "Article 423 of the Ordinance of Orleans" relating to notaries is not being observed in the colony, and that therefore the notaries must bind in chronological order by years all acts, binding the acts of each year separately "in a cover or volume," and label them by years. Procureurs of the king of ordinary jurisdiction were required to determine whether this ordinance was being followed.57

After Louisiana became a Spanish colony, notaries of the government and cabildo, royal notaries, and marine notaries were employed at the seat of government, while in the outlying posts the commandant had notarial authority. A proclamation by Unzaga, under the date of November 3, 1770, provided penalties on notaries for breach of trust, and the regulations of Morales, dated July 17, 1799, placed restrictions on their powers.58

50. La. A., 1855, #128; Rev. Stat., 1870, secs. 3149, 3150.
51. La. A., 1896, #53; ibid., 1910, #170.
52. La. A., 1877, E. S., #96, secs. 59, 60.
53. La. A., 1902, #181.
54. La. A., 1916, #229.
55. La. A., 1898, #170, sec. 51; ibid., 1928, #235; ibid., 1932, #194.
    *Though the notary public may from some points of view be considered a state rather than a parish official, we have included a brief essay on the notary, since by law his acts form a part of the parish archives.
56. Henry Plauche Dart, "The Legal Institutions of Louisiana," in La. Hist. Q., 1919, II, p. 85.
57. William K. Dart, (trans.), "Ordinances of 1717 Governing Notaries in Louisiana During French Colonial Period," in La. Hist. Q., 1927, X, pp. 82-85.
58. Edgar Grima, "The Notarial System in Louisiana," in La. Hist. Q., 1927, X, pp. 76, 77.

When the territory was ceded to the United States, the notaries continued to function as an integral part of the economic and political system. The early acts affecting them included the regulation of notarial fees,[59] the authorization to administer oaths,[60] the requirement to record protests,[61] and the recording of their acts in addition to depositing abstracts of such acts with the parish judge.[62] This latter provision was superseded in 1839 by requiring notaries to deposit their original acts, instead of extracts, with the recording official.[63]

The first state legislature provided that the governor appoint as many notaries public as were deemed necessary, "who shall remain in office during good behavior, but may be suspended by the supreme court until the next meeting of the state legislature."[64] A law of 1855 authorized the governor to appoint notaries, but limited their term of office to four years.[65] After the Civil War an attempt was made to change the office of notary public and make it a profession like an attorney at law.[66]

The duties and powers of notaries public were comprehensively defined in 1855. They were authorized to make inventories, appraisements, partitions, to receive wills, make protests, matrimonial contracts, conveyances, and generally all instruments of writing, to hold family meetings, meetings of creditors, and other duties of a similar character.[67]

Since 1855, a few laws have extended the powers of notaries. Among these is the provision that "oaths and acknowledgments in all cases may be taken or made by or before any notary public".[68] Another provision requires notaries to deposit in the office of the parish recorder "the original of all acts of sale, exchange, donation and mortgage on immovable property passed before them," except "that the foregoing provision shall not be so construed as embracing inventories or partitions or any other act performed by notaries or parish recorders under any order of court; but the original of all such acts, without being recorded, shall be returned to the court from which the order is issued".[69]

---

59. Or. Terr. A., 1805, XII.
60. Or. Terr. A., 1809, XXVII, sec. 3.
61. La. A., 1821, p. 44, sec. 1; ibid., 1355, #55, sec. 7.
62. La. A., 1822, p. 44, sec. 2.
63. La. A., 1839, #62, sec. 1; ibid., 1855, #261, sec. 12.
64. La. A., 1813, p. 136, sec. I; ibid., 1861, #117.
65. La. A., 1855, #261, sec. 1.
66. This act was passed, but inasmuch as it was signed by the governor during the recess of the legislature, it was not printed and bound with the acts. It was, however, inserted in Ray's Revised Statutes of 1870; cf. Grima, loc. cit., pp. 78, 79.
67. La. A., 1855, #261, sec. 2; Rev. Stat., 1870, secs. 2492, 2493.
68. La. A., 1877, E. S., #7.
69. La. A., 1890, #48, to amend art. 2251 of C. C., of 1870.

Original Notarial Acts

2. ACTS OF PEDRO DENYS DE LA RONDE, COMMANDANT, Sept. 14,
    1788-Nov. 5, 1802. 1 vol.
Original notarial acts passed before the Spanish commandant, including
acts of mortgage; acts of sale of land, property, and slaves; agreements;
marriages contracts; leases, and donations. Chron. arr. No index. Hdw.
in Spanish. Bound in paper in very poor condition; writing faded. 200
pp., 14 x 8 x 1.

3. [NOTARIAL ACTS AND RECORDS], 1806-14, 1818-46. 9 folders con-
    taining 51 vols.
Original notarial acts and records of the notaries and parish judges, including acts of sale; mortgages; exchange of slaves; marriage contracts;
family meetings; successions; leases; donations; and agreements. Chron.
arr. Indexed 1808-33, 1836-46 in vols., numer. by page nos., giving
type of act and names of parties involved; no index 1806-7, 1834-35.
Hdw. in Spanish, French, and English. Fragmentary; bound in paper in
very poor condition; writing faded. Vols. aver. 200 pp., 14 x 8 x 1.

4. [NOTARIAL ACTS OF LOUIS ALFRED DUCROS, RECORDER], Apr. 20,
    1846-May 28, 1853. 8 vols. in one bundle.
Notarial acts passed before Louis Alfred Ducros, recorder, including acts
of inventories of estates; family meetings; special mortgages; sales;
mortgages; sales of slaves; donations; confirmations of sales; promises
of sales; exchanges; procurations; marriage contracts; and partitions.
Chron. arr. No index. Hdw. in French, Spanish, and English (mostly in
French). Vols. aver. 200 pp., 14 x 8 x 1.

5. [NOTARIAL ACTS OF PHILLIPPE TOCA, RECORDER], June 28,
    1858-March 23, 1877. 10 vols. in one bundle.
Notarial acts passed before Phillippe Toca, recorder, including acts of
sale of land; sale of slaves to 1861; mortgages; donations; family meetings; inventories; declarations; bonds of parish officials; contracts;
transfers of mortgages; sheriff's sales; appointment of guardians; sales
under private signature; procurations; testaments; special mortgages;
declarations of domicile; protests of notes; powers of attorney; land
leases; agreements; charters; renunciation acts; acts relative to scrip
issued by the parish; mortgage releases; quietus; judgments; acts of succession; pledges on crops; and delinquent tax sales. Approx. chron. arr.
No index. Hdw. in French and English. Acts are fragmentary with many
pages missing. Vols. aver. 300 pp., 14 x 8 x 2.
    For other charters, see entries 6, 7, 13, 15.

6. NOTARIAL ACTS, JAS. D. ST. ALEXANDRE, July 22, 1892-May 16,
    1924. 5 vols.
Notarial acts passed before James D. St. Alexandre, including acts of
sale of real and personal property; conventional, chattel, and judicial
mortgages; credit sales; sales of property with mortgages; charters,
amendments to charters, and dissolutions of charters; certificates of
mortgages; powers of attorney; family meetings, partitions, inventories
of estates, authorizations of court for inventories; meetings of creditors;

petitions for respite; agreements; leases; land maps; exchanges of property; and protests. Chron. arr. No index 1892-1900, 1905-11. Indexed
in vols. 1901-4, 1912-15, alph. by first letter of surname of both parties, chron. thereunder; indexed in vols. 1916-24, alph. by first letter
of surname of first party, chron. thereunder. Hdw., 1892-1900; hdw. and
typed, 1910-24. Aver. 300 pp., 16 x 11 x 3.
        For other chattel mortgages, see entries 7, 11, 12; for other chart-
ers, see entries 5, 7, 13, 15.

    7. NOTARIAL ACTS, 1849-1903, 1905--. 44 vols. 1st vol. 1849-1903,
        titled Miscellaneous Acts.
Original notarial acts of cash and credit sales; sales of chattel property; crop liens and privileges; indentures; conventional, chattel, and
judicial mortgages; certificates of mortgages; powers of attorney; police
jury ordinances; charters, amendments, and dissolutions of charters; certificates of redemption of land sold for taxes and bid in for the state;
assignments of oil, gas, and mineral rights; certificates of acknowledgments; oil, gas, and mineral leases; federal land grants; and property
maps. Chron. arr. Indexed alph. in vol. 1849-1903 by first letter of
surname of both parties, chron. thereunder. No index, 1905--. Hdw.,
1849-1903; hdw., typed, and photostat, 1905--. Aver. 300 pp., 16 x 11 x 3
        For additional oil, gas, and mineral leases, see entry 9; for other
chattel mortgages, see entries 6, 11, 12; for other charters, see entries
5, 6, 13, 15.

    8. [ORIGINAL SHERIFF'S TAX SALES], 1908--. In Copies of Certifi-
        cates, entry 53.
Original sheriff's tax sales giving name of sheriff, date advertised and
paper advertised in, place and date of sale, the period during which advertisement appeared in newspaper, the owner of property, description of
property, list of various taxes due, the day, hour, and place at which
the property was offered for sale, the amount bid, to whom sold; statement that property sold may be redeemed by taxpayer at any time within
three years from date of sheriff's sale upon payment of price paid by
vendee, with five per cent penalty, and one per cent interest per month
until redeemed, and all costs added; date, signatures of sheriff and witnesses. Chron. arr. by dates of sale. No index. Typed and hdw. on
printed forms.
        For record of sheriff's tax sales, see entries 16, 17, 113.

    9. CONVEYANCE RECORD [Original Oil Leases, Assignments, and Min-
        eral Leases], March 31, 1922-November 19, 1932. 1 vol. (30).
Original leases giving date agreement was made, name of lessor, name of
lessee, amount paid lessor for granting lease, description of land leased, location by section, township, and range, terms of lease, amount to
be paid annually, manner of payment, date of termination of lease if no
operations are begun, and amount of rental to be paid for the privilege
of deferring the commencement of operations, date attested, and signatures of lessor and witnesses. Chron. arr. by filing date. No index.
Typed, and typed on printed forms. 600 pp., 18 x 12 x 3.
        For additional oil, gas, and mineral leases, see entry 7.

10. ₍LEASES₎, 1924--. 1 steel file drawer.
Original leases, cancellation of leases, and sale of leases, giving date
of instrument, names of lessor and lessee, description of property leased, terms, signatures of lessor, lessee, witnesses, and notary, and date
filed and recorded. Chron. arr. No index. Typed. 5 x 11 x 17.

11. ₍Original₎ CHATTEL MORTGAGES, 1926--. 5 steel file drawers.
Original acts of chattel mortgage, and sale and chattel mortgage, giving
date of instrument, names of notary, mortgagor and mortgagee, amount of
mortgage, date due, description of property mortgaged, signatures of
principals, witnesses, and notary, date filed, date recorded, and date
cancelled. Chron. arr. No index. Typed on printed forms. 5 x 11 x 17.
For other chattel mortgages, see entries 6, 7, 12.

12. TRAPPERS CHATTEL MORTGAGES TO U. S. A., 1937--. 1 steel file
    box.
Original chattel mortgages in favor of the United States, issued through
the United States Department of Agriculture, pursuant to authority vested in Secretary of Agriculture by Executive Order No. 7530, Dec. 31,
1936, giving date, name of notary, name of client, location and description of land where trapping of furs is carried on, name of owner, total
sum advanced, date client subscribed his promissory notes, when due,
amount of interest, name of security, location of security property,
description of property securing loan, name of place where notarial act
is passed, name of person before whom the act was passed, signatures of
client, witnesses and notary public. Chron. arr. by date filed. No index. Hdw. and typed on mimeographed forms. 11 x 5 x 17.
For other chattel mortgages, see entries 6, 7, 11.

13. ₍Original₎ CHARTERS AND BUILDING CONTRACTS, 1926--. 1 steel
    file box.
Original acts of charters, amendments to charters, and building contracts.
Charters give name or title of corporation or association, a description
of the purposes for which it is established; the nature of the business
or activity to be carried on; the name of the officers on whom citation
may be served; if a stock corporation, the amount of capital stock, the
number of shares, the value of each share, and the time when, and manner
in which, payment on stock subscribed shall be made; the mode in which
the election of directors or other officers shall be conducted, the
length of time during which the corporation shall exist, and the mode of
liquidation. Building contracts give names and addresses of contracting
parties, amount of contract, description of building or improvements to
be made, signatures of contracting parties, witnesses, and notary public.
Not arr. No index. Typed and typed on printed forms. 11 x 5 x 17.
For other charters, see entries 5, 6, 7, 15.

14. ₍Original₎ LIEN AND PRIVILEGE, 1925-32. 1 steel file box.
Original acts of lien and privilege against property, real and chattel,
giving name of deponent, name of person(s) indebted to deponent, amount
of debt, description of property or chattel for which debt was incurred,
name of owner, signature of deponent, date subscribed, signature of
notary, rubber stamped on each act by the clerk of court and ex officio

recorder, giving the book and page no. of record in which the above acts have been recorded, the date recorded and filed. Contains also two notices of tax liens and two certificates of discharges of tax liens under internal revenue law, giving U. S. Internal Revenue District, city, date, name of taxpayer, residence or place of business, nature of income, taxable period, amount of tax assessed, additional (penalty) tax assessed, date assessment list received, signature of collector, notation of recorder when filed, and the book and page number where recorded. Certificates of discharge give number, name of district, city, date, name and residence of persons assessed, nature of tax, taxable period, amount of tax satisfied, signature of collector, and notation by recorder where and when recorded. Chron. arr. No index. Hdw., typed, and typed on printed forms. 11 x 5 x 17.

15. CLERK'S NOTARIAL ACTS, 1924--. 1 steel file drawer.
Original notarial acts executed by the clerk of court and ex officio recorder, including sale of property, cash and credit; succession acts, transfers and dedications, charters, inventories in successions, conventional mortgages, oaths of office, sheriff's sales, dation en paiment. In some cases blueprint maps of property involved are attached to notarial acts. Chron. arr. by date filed. No index. Typed, and typed on printed forms. 11 x 15 x 18.
    For other charters, see entries 5, 6, 7, 13.

Real and Personal Property and Rights

Conveyances

16. CONVEYANCE RECORD, Feb. 8, 1883--. 27 vols. (16-29, 31-43,
            and dated). Missing: vols. 1-15; destroyed in courthouse fire.
Record of conveyances including sale of land, property, chattels, sheriff's sales for taxes; donations inter vivos; judgments; rights of way; declarations of titles; divisions and exchanges of property; sheriff's succession sales; sales of hereditary rights; patents of lands by United States; redemptions of property from taxes; sales with mortgage; assignments of leases; quit claims; sales to State for taxes; dation en paiment; and mineral leases. Some conveyances previous to 1883 which were destroyed by fire are recorded de novo in vol. 16. Chron. arr. by dates recorded. Indexed alph. in vols. by first letter of surname of both parties, chron. thereunder, giving type of instrument, and page no. of record. Hdw. 1883-Aug. 11, 1926; typed thereafter; some on printed forms. Aver. 600 pp., 18 x 12 x 3.
    For original acts of conveyance, see entries 6, 7, 9, 10, 15; for additional donations, see entries 44, 45.

17. ₍Sheriff's₎ DEED BOOK, July 19, 1866-Sept. 2, 1922. 4 vols.
            Discontinued, subsequently recorded only in Conveyance Record, entry 16.
Record of sheriff's sales made by virtue of writs of seizure, and sale,

by order of sale in successions, and by writs of fieri facias, giving
the name of the person whose property was sold, name of purchaser, court
rendering judgment, date, name of sheriff to whom writ was directed, number and title of suit, statement of sheriff that he had served copy of
notice to pay, date property was seized, date of advertisement and in
what newspaper, date, hour, and place sold, amount of highest bid, to
whom sold, description of property, amount retained for costs, amount
turned over to plaintiff, name of sheriff, and date filed. Chron. arr.
No index. Hdw. Aver. 400 pp., 18 x 12 x 2.
    For original sheriff's deeds, see entries 5, 8, 15; for record of
sheriff's tax sales, see entry 113; for duplicate recordings, see entry
16.

Conveyance Maps

    18. MAP, ST. BERNARD PARISH, 1896. 1 map.
Political and land tenure map of St. Bernard Parish, showing property of
Lake Borgne Levee Board. Smith and Kaiser, artists; publisher and place
of publication not given. Scale, 3 in. equals 1 mile. Printed in col-
ors. Very poor condition. 72 x 108.

    19. N. O. TERMINAL CO., July 6, 1921. 1 map.
Land tenure map of subdivisions of property of the New Orleans Terminal
Co., in St. Bernard Parish. Identified with an act of sale dated Sept.
3, 1921. Blueprint. Scale, 1 in. equals 200 feet. Lacy Moore, Engi-
neer and Surveyor. Publisher and place of publication not given.
40 x 92.

    20. MAP SHOWING SUBDIVISION OF PARTS [of] T.[ownship] 12 S.[outh]
        R.[ange] 12 E.[ast] and T.[ownship] 13 S.[outh] R.[ange] 12
        E.[ast] IN ST. BERNARD & ORLEANS PARISHES, April 7, 1936. 1
        map.
Land tenure map, showing lots located in the above area. Black and
white. Scale, not given. Victor Hawkins, artist, New Orleans, La.
68 x 39.

    21. [LAND BELONGING TO ALCIDE H. GUTIERREZ], July 28, 1937. 1 map.
Land tenure map showing land belonging to the above person. Black and
white. Scale, 1 in., equals 400 feet. Victor E. Hawkins, artist, New Orleans, La. 7 x 21½.

    22. MAP OF PART OF POYDRAS PLANTATION IN ST. BERNARD PARISH,
        T.[ownship] 14, S.[outh] - R.[ange] 13 E.[ast] - SHOWING LOT
        12 NEW, OLD N-1-4, Dec. 26, 1924. 1 map.
Land tenure map of part of the Poydras plantation. Blueprint. Scale, 1
in. equals 200 feet. J. W. Stephens, artist, New Orleans, La. 9 x 17.

23. MAP OF PART OF POYDRAS PLANTATION, ST. BERNARD PARISH, T.ｌownshipｌ 13, S.ｌouthｌ - R.ｌangeｌ 13 E.ｌastｌ SHOWING RESUBDIVISION OF LOTS C-19-21-22 CONTAINING 0.389 ACRES, TO BE KNOWN AS LOT C-48. July 16, 1924. 1 map.
Land tenure map of part of Poydras plantation. Blueprint. Scale, 1 in. equals 50 feet. J. A. Stephens, artist, New Orleans, La. 12 x 10.

24. M G, 4-5-6-7 and 8 POYDRAS PLANTATION IN ST. BERNARD PARISH, LA., July 16, 1924. 2 maps.
Land tenure maps of part of Poydras plantation in township 35, range 14 east, containing 50.00 acres clear land and 47.00 acres wooded land; total 97.00 acres. Blueprint. Scale, 1 in. equals 300 feet. J. W. Stephens, artist, New Orleans, La. 10 x 14.

25. MAP OF PART OF POYDRAS PLANTATION IN ST. BERNARD PARISH, Dec. 20, 1923. 1 map.
Land tenure map of part of Poydras plantation in township 14 south, range 13 east, showing re-survey of Section A and part of Section T, now called division R, changes being incident to crevasse in levee. Blueprint. Scale, 1 in. equals 200 feet. J. W. Stephens, artist, New Orleans, La. 22½ x 14.

26. ｌMAP OF POYDRAS SUBDIVISIONｌ, March 23, 1923. 1 map.
Land tenure map of Poydras subdivision. Map states "4 and 4A, Proces verbal (4) A-.88 acres (4)-2.72 acres. Tract 1 ▪ 0.16 acres, No. 2, 0.88. 2.56 taken by levee, road and pond." Blueprint. Scale, 1 in. equals 50 feet. C. A. Robert, artist, New Orleans, La. 16 x 22.

27. MAP SHOWING RE-SUBDIVISION OF SEC. F. OF POYDRAS PLANTATION IN ST. BERNARD PARISH, March 21, 1923. 2 items containing 3 maps; also 1 duplicate.
Land tenure map of part of Poydras plantation. Blueprint. Scale, 1 in. equals 200 feet. J. W. Stephens, artist, New Orleans, La. 17½ x 20½.

28. MAP OF PART OF POYDRAS PLANTATION IN ST. BERNARD PARISH, n. d. 1 map.
Land tenure map of part of Poydras plantation in township 14 south, range 13 east, showing subdivision R composed of parts of sections A. R. and T. as per map dated February 3, 1921, and subsequent subdivision thereof as sections R 4-5-6-7 and 8. Area of section R, clear land 17 acres, wet wooded 220 acres, prairie, 160 acres. Lot A3A 1.16-A5 ▪ 5.94. Total 404.10 acres. Blueprint. Scale, 1 in. equals 200 feet. J. W. Stephens, artist, New Orleans, La. 41 x 26.

29. HIGHLAND ADDITION TO BORGNEMOUTH, n. d. 1 map.
Land tenure map of a subdivision in St. Bernard Parish identified with an act of sale by Ferdinand Lepage to Louis Anthony Meraux, M. D., passed April 28, 1931. Lots in this addition are 20 x 80 feet. Photostat. Scale, 1 in. equals 50 feet. 8 x 16.

III. CLERK OF COURT

During the period of the county system of government, the clerk of the county court was appointed by the governor.1 When St. Bernard Parish was created in 1807, at the same time that the parish court came into existence, the judge of the parish court was obliged to serve as his own clerk.2 When the district court was created in 1813, a clerk of court was provided for each parish. He served in ex officio capacity as clerk of the parish court from 1813 to 1820.3 In this latter year, the legislature abolished the office of clerk of court as far as it related to the parish court of St. Bernard Parish,4 and ordered the parish judge to assume again the duties of clerk of his own court. But in 1833 the St. Bernard Parish judge was given authority to appoint a clerk of his court.5 The clerk of the district court served in ex officio capacity as clerk of the second parish court from 1868 to 1879,6 as clerk of court of appeal from 1879 to 1900,7 and as ex officio clerk of the juvenile court.8

The clerk of the district court was appointed by the district judge until the adoption of the Constitution of 1845.9 Since this time the clerk of court has been elected for a term of four years. Until 1904, vacancies in the office of clerk had been filled by appointment by the district judge. Since this time the governor fills vacancies in the office of clerk when the unexpired term is less than one year, but by special election called by him if the unexpired term be longer.10

The clerk of court is empowered to appoint as many deputies as he thinks are necessary, subject to the approval of the district judge.11

Fees and charges of the clerk of court are fixed by law.12 He is given authority to demand from parties offering to file suits in the district court the sum of $10 as a cash deposit to cover the costs to be

---

1. Or. Terr. A., 1805, XXV, sec. 2.

2. Or. Terr. A., 1807, I, sec. 10.

3. La. A., 1813, p. 18, sec. 22.

4. La. A., 1820, p. 32, sec. 1.

5. La. A., 1833, p. 93.

6. La. A., 1868, #51, sec. 4.

7. Const., 1879, art. 121. This article also makes the clerk of court ex officio recorder and notary public.

8. Const., 1913, art. 118; Const., 1921, art. VII, sec. 53.

9. La. A., 1813, p. 18, sec 22.

10. Const., 1845, art. 82; Const., 1852, art 79; La. A., 1855, #56; Const., 1861, art. 79; Const., 1864, art. 80; La. A., 1867, #134; Const., 1868, art.

83; Const., 1879, art. 121; Const., 1898, art. 122; La. A., 1904, #139; Const., 1913, art. 122; Const., 1921, art. VII, sec. 6.

11. La. A., 1846, #96, sec. 18; ibid., 1853, #329, sec. 7; ibid., 1855, #56, sec 12; Const., 1879, art. 123; Const., 1898, art. 124; Const., 1913, art. 124; Const., 1921, art. VII, sec. 67; La. A., 1924, #204, sec. 10.

12. Or. Terr. A., 1805, XXXVI, sec. 2; La. A., 1813, p. 176, sec. 1; ibid., 1814, p. 108; ibid., 1855, #122, sec. 11; ibid., 1898, #203, secs. 2, 6; ibid., 1936, #334.

incurred. During the life of the second parish court he was allowed to demand a cash deposit of $5 for costs of suits brought in that court.[13]

The duties and functions of the clerk of court when the office was created in 1813 were to be the same, until otherwise prescribed, as those fulfilled by the clerk of the late superior court.[14] These were, briefly, to give copies of the court papers to any individual demanding them;[15] to keep a file of newspapers in which were inserted official and public notices;[16] to make out citations and transcripts of petitions when requested by the petitioner or his attorney; to issue process to the sheriff when the plaintiff requests a trial by jury; to issue writs of attachment, fiere facias, execution, distringas, and all other writs which the court was empowered to issue; to issue summons for witnesses; to enter all judgments on the minutes of the court; and to keep a book for entering a docket or short note of all judgments for the payment of money.[17] The clerk was also authorized to take affidavits for holding debtors to special bail and for attaching the property of debtors.[18]

During the period until the second constitution, other duties were prescribed by statute. These were: to issue certificates of day attendance and mileage to jurors and witnesses;[19] to record in a well bound book (within six months after the rendition of final judgment) the petitions, answers, orders of the court, interlocutory judgments, together with final judgments of the court; to record proceedings in cases appealed and proceedings in successions;[20] and, finally, to aid in the drawing of jurors.[21]

The powers of the clerk were outlined in full in 1846. He was empowered to issue writs of arrest, attachment, sequestration, and provisional seizure; to issue commissions to take testimony; to grant orders affixing seals and taking inventories; to call family meetings; to take orders for the probate and execution of wills; to grant marriage licenses; and to issue citations to warrantors. Furthermore, he was authorized to grant orders for sale of property in successions; to assume the administration of small successions for which no person applied; to send annually a list of vacant estates to the state treasurer; and to call family meetings to nominate tutors in the event that no one volunteered to undertake that responsibility. In all cases of opposition to any order granted or motion filed, the clerk was ordered to place such opposition on the docket and issue a copy of the motion to the opposite party. He was also required to record all proceedings in successions.[22]

Since this time the duties and powers of the clerk have been

---

13. La. A., 1877, E. S., #15.   3.

14. La. A., 1813, p. 18, sec. 22.   19. La. A., 1823, p. 58.

15. Or. Terr. A., 1805, XVI, sec.   20. La. A., 1825, p. 212, sec.
    3.   1.

16. Or. Terr. A., 1805, XVII,   21. La. A., 1840, #32, secs. 2,
    secs. 1, 3.   3; see Jury Commission, p. 85.

17. Or. Terr. A., 1805, XXVI.   22. La. A., 1846, #96; ibid.,
18. Or. Terr. A., 1805, V, sec.   1850, #141, secs. 2, 3.

re-stated at intervals, and augmented in many acts of the legislature.[23]
In addition to those powers and duties already mentioned, the clerk records bonds, particularly those of curators, tutors, and administrators;[24] administers oaths;[25] makes transcripts of cases appealed to the
supreme court;[26] causes the bonds of tutors and curators to be recorded
in the mortgage office;[27] grants orders of injunction in the absence of
the district judge;[28] fixes the amount of bonds, and appoints experts
and appraisers.[29] He keeps a record of the registry of the court, in
which he records and indexes every judgment ordering the deposit or
withdrawal of funds belonging to minors, interdicts, absentees, or persons unknown.[30]

When the clerk of the district court was ex officio clerk of the
second parish court, 1868-79, he was required to keep three dockets,
probate, civil, and criminal; to issue citations, copies of petitions,
executions, writs of seizure and sale, injunctions, attachments, provisional seizure, arrests, and all other writs or orders of the parish
court.[31]

The clerk has certain judicial powers in cases in which the district
court has concurrent jurisdiction with the justices of the peace. He
may render judgment and grant orders for writs in the exercise of this
power. In such cases the clerk notes in a book known as "Clerk's Book"
the title and number of the suit, in addition to docketing it in the
regular court docket, and records the defaults taken before him, as
well as judgments rendered by him.[32]

The clerk also makes a record of the proces verbal of the coron-
ers inquests, the originals of which are filed in his office;[33] records
all marriage licenses, which he, or his deputy, only may issue;[34] sends
to the state board of health statistics on divorce;[35] and an annual
abridged statement of all marriage licenses.[36] He records certificates
of osteopaths,[37] veterinarians,[38] architects,[39] civil engineers and

---

23. La. A., 1853, #329; ibid.,
    1855, #56; ibid., 1857, #281;
    ibid., 1861, #220; ibid.,
    1867, #141; ibid., 1869,
    #110; ibid., 1880, #106;
    ibid., 1882, #43; ibid.,
    1884, #75; ibid., 1894, #13;
    ibid., 1921, E. S., #41;
    ibid., 1924, #204.
24. La. A., 1855, #56, sec. 16;
    ibid., #253, sec. 6.
25. La. A., 1853, #329, sec. 1.
26. La. A., 1855, #121, sec. 27.
27. La. A., 1855, #253, sec. 6.
28. La. A., 1855, #262, sec. 1.
29. La. A., 1861, #220.

30. La. A., 1920, #246.
31. La. A., 1868, #51, sec. 4;
    ibid., 1869, #110, sec. 1.
32. La. A., 1922, #47, sec. 2.
33. La. A., 1875, #27, sec. 1.
34. La. A., 1912, #104; ibid.,
    1934, #148.
35. La. A., 1908, #307, sec. 1;
    ibid., 1936, #249.
36. La. A., 1910, #125.
37. La. A., 1908, #185, sec. 6;
    ibid., 1918, #193.
38. La. A., 1908, #202, secs.
    11, 12.
39. La. A., 1910, #231, sec. 7.

surveyors,[40] registered nurses,[41] medical and dental certificates,[42] and the discharge papers of soldiers, sailors, marines.[43] He receives and records the proces verbal of elections to levy special taxes;[44] registers the names of purchasers of rural mortgage bonds;[45] records the acts of incorporation of non-trading corporations;[46] proceedings in regard to the issuance of bonds by parishes and municipalities;[47] and registers the names and addresses of persons designated in business licenses.[48] He is authorized to keep an alphabetical index of persons conducting a business under an assumed name;[49] and lists of persons convicted of crimes punishable at hard labor or imprisonment in the penitentiary.[50]

The clerk's office is also a depository for filing duplicate registry of voters;[51] trade-marks or devices on seltzer or mineral water bottles;[52] names of agents of foreign corporations;[53] inventories of stocks of jewelry to be sold at auction;[54] contractors' claim bonds;[55] copies of bonds of real estate agents;[56] and statements of expenses of candidates for public office.[57]

The clerk has, at times, discharged other functions. From 1815 to 1846 he was declared to be stamper of weights and measures in the parish.[58] From 1817 to 1819 he received and made three copies of the assessment rolls.[59] The clerk of the court has been authorized since 1850, to convene the police jury in the event of a vacancy in the office of the president.[60] The clerk is also ex officio member of the jury commission.[61] During Reconstruction the clerk of the district court, with the sheriff and recorder, served as a board of parish assessors for the purpose of fixing the valuation of property assessed.[62]

---

40. La. A., 1908, #308, sec. 7; ibid., 1914, #200, sec. 6.
41. La. A., 1912, #138, sec. 6.
42. La. A., 1914, #56, sec. 9; ibid., 1928, #253, sec. 12.
43. La. A., 1921, E. S., #104.
44. La. A., 1910, #256, sec. 15.
45. La. A., 1914, #176, sec. 11.
46. La. A., 1914, #254, sec. 2.
47. La. A., 1916, #96.
48. La. A., 1916, #159.
49. La. A., 1918, #64, sec. 3.
50. The clerk keeps this list so that the registrar of voters may strike the names of such persons from the registration books; cf. La. A., 1921, E. S., #122, sec. 31.
51. La. A., 1869, #132; ibid., 1873, #155, sec. 9; Const.,

1898, art. 197, sec. 5.
52. La. A., 1896, #120.
53. La. A., 1912, #194, sec. 1.
54. La. A., 1924, #245, sec. 2.
55. La. A., 1926, #246.
56. La. A., 1928, #269, sec. 2.
57. La. A., 1916, #130, sec. 73; ibid., 1932, #160.
58. La. A., 1814-15, p. 24, sec. 4; ibid., 1846, #122, sec. 2.
59. La. A., 1817, p. 170, secs. 2, 3; ibid., 1818, p. 190, sec. 8; repealed by La. A., 1819, p. 130, sec. 1.
60. La. A., 1850, #37; Rev. Stat., 1870, sec. 2733.
61. See Jury Commission, p. 85.
62. La. A., 1868, #196, sec. 20; ibid., 1869, #114, sec. 43(44); ibid., 1871, #42, sec. 40.

Clerk of Court - Marriage Records

Marriage Records

60. DOCTOR CERTIFICATES, 1925--. 1 steel file drawer.
Certificates issued by doctors to male applicants for marriage licenses,
giving date, statement that applicant is free from diseases, and signature of doctor. No arr. No index. Hdw. on printed forms.
11 x 14 x 18.

61. [MARRIAGE LICENSE STATISTICS], 1937--. 1 cardboard box.
Data required by law in order to obtain and put on record questions
answered by party making application for marriage license, giving date
of license, full name of man, residence, color, age last birthday, occu-
pation, name of mother, whether living or dead, name of father, whether
living or dead, residence of each, whether applicant was previously mar-
ried, if so, name of former wife, whether dead, alive, or divorced, relationship of parties, if any. Same information as above on woman, signature of applicant, date subscribed, signature of clerk, date of marriage,
place, and name of official. Chron. arr. No index. Hdw. on printed
forms. 9 x 11 x 15.

62. MARRIAGE BONDS, 1831-46, 1847-52, 1866-1905. 1 vol. and 1
        folder containing 4 vols. (dated). Discontinued. Title
        varies: Marriage Record.
Bonds posted by male contracting party of a marriage at time of application, to be forfeited in the event that there exist a legal impediment,
giving name of male contracting party as principal, name of surety,
amount of bond, name of party to whom obligated, date, and signatures of
principal, surety, and clerk of court. Prior to 1876, consent of parents
to marriage also included, giving date, name of contracting party, name
of parent, tutor or guardian and in cases of minors, age of contracting
party. Chron. arr. No index. Hdw. on printed forms. Records prior
to 1876 in poor condition, no binding, writing faded, paper poor, having
been watersoaked. Vols. aver. 400 pp., two bonds to a page, 14 x 8 x 2.

63. MARRIAGE CERTIFICATES, June 12, 1877--. 21 vols. (dated).
        Title varies: Marriage Licenses.
Duplicate of licenses issued to a legal officiant to celebrate marriage
between contracting parties, giving name of state, parish, judicial district, officiant, names and residences of contracting parties, and both
parents of each, date license issued, and signature of clerk of court.
Prior to 1915, names of parents of contracting parties not given. Chron.
arr. No index. Hdw. on printed forms. Aver. 500 pp., two certificates
to a page, 10 x 18 x 3.

64. MARRIAGE RECORD, 1835-50, 1876--. 11 vols. (First vol. not
        numbered, then 1, 2, 2A, 3-9, and dated). Title varies:
        Record of Marriage and Births.
Record of certificates of marriage, giving date celebrated, names of
contracting parties, witnesses, officiant, date, and signature of recorder. Prior to 1850, records are duplicate originals and give name of parents of contracting parties along with the above information. An occasional baptismal, birth, and death certificates is recorded in these

records. Chron. arr. No index 1835-50, 1924-28; indexed 1876-1917 in
entry 65; indexed in vol. 1917-23, 1929--, alph. by first letter of surname of both parties, chron. thereunder. Hdw. 1835-1922; typed 1923-29;
hdw. on printed forms 1930-36, typed 1936--. Aver. 500 pp.,
16 x 12 x 2½.

    65. INDEX, RECORD OF BIRTHS, DEATHS AND MARRIAGES, 1876-1917. 1
        vol. (1).
Alphabetical index to marriage records, entry 64, by first letter of surname of both parties, chron. thereunder, giving name of opposite party
and page number of record. Occasional birth or death records included
as in volume of which this is an index. Hdw. 26 pp., 15 x 10 x ¼.

Oaths and Bonds

    66. OATHS AND BONDS, July 4, 1892--. 1 steel file box.
Original oaths and bonds of parish officials. Oaths give name of person
swearing to oath, duties to be performed, date subscribed, signatures of
incumbent and clerk before whom oath was taken. Bonds give names of
principal and surety, amount of bond posted by each, condition of obli-
gation, name of official, date subscribed, signatures of principal,
surety, and witnesses. Notation on each oath and bond by clerk stating
the date same was recorded, and the volume number and page of mortgage
record in which recorded. Not arr. No index. Hdw. and typed on printed forms. 11 x 5 x 17.
    For record of oaths and bonds, see entry 47.

Miscellaneous

    67. EXPENSE ACCOUNTS [of Candidates for Public Office], Apr. 22,
        1920-May 7, 1924. 1 steel file box.
Affidavits of candidates for public office as to expense incurred, giving the amount spent, if any, signature of candidate, date subscribed,
signature of notary public, and date filed with clerk of court. Chron.
arr. by filing dates. No index. Typed. 11 x 5 x 17.

    68. NOTICE EMPLOYERS INSURANCE [Employers' Notices of Compliance
        with Sec. 22 of Act 247 of 1920], 1920--. 1 steel file box,
        last notice filed 1929.
Cards and certificates filed with the clerk of court in compliance with
the above act. Cards state that the employer has complied with the act,
giving signature of employer, place at which card was dated, date filed
with clerk and recorded in mortgage record. Also contains daily report
of Louisiana Workmen's compensation policies filed on behalf of employ-
ers by their insurance companies, giving name of employer, street address, nature of employer's business, and policy number, notation when
filed and recorded with clerk of court. Not arr. No index. Hdw. on
printed forms. 11 x 5 x 17.
    For record, see entry 47.

X. SHERIFF

In colonial Louisiana the officer who served in a capacity similar to the sheriff was the "alguacil."[1] When, after the Louisiana Purchase, counties were erected these duties were discharged by the county sheriff. When the first civil parishes were created all parish functions were concentrated in the parish judge.[2] The office of parish sheriff was created in 1810 by an act of the territorial legislature which stated "there shall be a sheriff appointed in each of the parishes of the Territory, except Orleans Parish." A provision was added, however, that the parish judge continue to discharge the functions of the sheriff until that officer be appointed and in office.[3]

The Constitution of 1812 provided that the parish sheriff be appointed by the governor, and the legislature meeting in the following year fixed his term of office at three years,[4] but in 1825 his term was reduced to two years.[5] The second constitution made the sheriff an elective officer, and the term two years.[6] The office has been elective to the present day, except that since 1879, the term has been four years.[7]

Vacancies in the office have always been filled by appointees of the governor,[8] but in 1913 the governor was authorized to fill such vacancies only when the unexpired term was less than one year. If the unexpired term were more than a year, then the governor was ordered to call a special election to fill the vacancy.[9]

The sheriff has been empowered to appoint the necessary deputies since 1813.[10] A law of 1902 directed him to appoint one or more special deputies for police duty in unincorporated towns, villages, or in any ward, when requested to do so by six or more citizens,[11] but an act of 1920 provided that the appointment and compensation of additional deputies have the approval of the district judge and of the president of the police jury in order to determine the necessity for the additional expense.[12] The law governing the appointment of deputies which is in effect today empowers the sheriff to appoint, but the appointees must have the approval of the superintendent of the state bureau of criminal investigation and identification. It is mandatory for the superintendent to approve five appointees, but above this number approval is discretionary.[13]

1. Carleton, op. cit., p. 61.
2. Or. Terr. A., 1807, I.
3. Or. Terr. A., 1810, VIII, secs. 1, 6.
4. Const., 1812, art. III, sec. 9; La. A., 1813, p. 18.
5. La. A., 1825, p. 112.
6. Const., 1845, art. 83.
7. Const., 1852, art. 80; La. A., 1855, #301; Const., 1864, art. 84; Const., 1868, art. 93; Const., 1879, art. 119; Const., 1898, art. 119; Const., 1913,

art. 119; Const., 1921, art. VII, secs. 63, 69.
8. Const., 1812, art. III, sec. 10.
9. See footnotes 5, 6.
10. La. A., 1813, p. 142, sec. 7; ibid., 1855, #301, sec. 6; Rev. Stat., 1870, sec. 3542.
11. La. A., 1902, #27.
12. La. A., 1920, #156, sec. 2; ibid., 1924, #86.
13. La. A., 1934, 3rd E.S., #27.

The fees, commissions, and salary of the sheriff have been regulated by
law and before he takes office he must post a good and sufficient
bond.[14]

The duties of the county sheriff, as prescribed by the legislative
council of 1805-6, were to execute all orders and writs directed to him
either by the county or superior courts; to record all sales made by
him in a book kept for that purpose; to issue a conveyance on every judicial sale made by him; to take charge of all persons committed to
prison for any offenses against the territory; to attend the sessions of
the county and superior courts either in person or by deputy; to preserve the peace and apprehend for punishment all disturbers thereof; and
to summon a posse comitatus in case of riot.[15] Whenever a person was
committed to the custody of the county sheriff for a capital or other
offense exclusively cognizable in the superior court, it became his duty
to deliver the person into the hands of the sheriff in the city of New
Orleans.[16] The sheriff also acted as tax collector,[17] was ordered to
take a census of the inhabitants,[18] and to assist the justices of the
peace in receiving and counting votes cast in the election of representatives.[19]

When the office of sheriff was set up for the parishes, this officer was empowered to execute all warrants, orders, writs, or other process of the parish judge; to be "keeper of the jail"; to form a list of
inhabitants eligible for jury service, and to summon such persons when
necessary.[20]

The duties of the sheriff of today do not vary substantially from
those outlined by the legislature before Louisiana became a state. As
new courts were created he was authorized to perform the same duties for
them as the county and parish sheriff had performed for the courts of
the territorial period.[21]

In a parish in which an execution is to take place, it is the duty
of the sheriff or duly authorized deputy, or competent person selected
by him, to execute the convict in conformity with the death warrant and
command issued to him by the governor under the seal of the state of

14. La. A., 1814, p. 108; Const.,
    1879, art. 118; Const., 1898,
    art. 119; Const., 1913, art.
    119; Const., 1921, art. VII,
    sec. 65.
15. Or. Terr. A., 1805, XXV, sec.
    14; ibid., L, sec. 49.
16. Or. Terr. A., 1805, XLIV, sec. 5.
17. Or. Terr. A., 1805, XLIII, sec.
    2. The duties of the sheriff
    as tax collector have been
    treated separately, see essay
    p. 110.
18. Or. Terr. A., 1806, VIII, sec.

1.
19. Or. Terr. A., 1806, XIX,
    sec. 4.
20. Or. Terr. A., 1810, VIII,
    sec. 1; ibid., X.
21. La. A., 1813, p. 18, sec. 23;
    ibid., p. 142, sec. 1; ibid.,
    1855, #301; ibid., 1868, #61,
    secs. 1, 3; ibid., #123, secs.
    1-3; Const., 1879, art. 106;
    Const., 1898, art. 106; Const.
    1913, art. 106; Const., 1921,
    art. VII, sec. 28.

Louisiana. Every sentence of death must be executed at the parish prison of the parish in which the crime was committed, or in the parish to
which venue has been changed. Said execution is by hanging. Every execution of a death sentence takes place in the presence of the sheriff
or one of his deputies, the coroner, or a practicing physician designated by him, a priest or minister, if the convict so requests, and of not
less than five nor more than seven witnesses, all citizens of the state
of Louisiana. It is mandatory upon the sheriff, or his deputy, to make
proces verbal of an execution immediately thereafter, which proces verbal is attested by the sheriff, or his deputy performing the execution,
and all of the witnesses. The proces verbal, when so signed, is filed
with the clerk of court where the sentence has been imposed.[22]

In 1868, the duties and powers of the sheriff of St. Bernard Parish was practically usurped by the Metropolitan Police, who were in existence from 1868 until 1877, when they were abolished by legislative
enactment.

In addition to those duties already mentioned, the sheriff is
obliged to convey insane persons to the state insane asylum;[23] to receive into custody United States prisoners delivered to him by the mar-
shal of the district of Louisiana;[24] to convey lepers to the leper
home;[25] and to deliver prisoners sentenced to hard labor to the state
penitentiary.[26] He is authorized to employ prisoners for work on public roads, levees, streets, public buildings or public works inside or
outside the prison;[27] to purchase and keep "track or trailing dogs" for
the purpose of tracking and pursuing fugitives from justice;[28] to purchase and possess machine guns,[29] tear gas, tear gas guns, bullet proof
vests, and other law enforcement equipment;[30] and to take the finger-
prints of any person who is believed to have committed a felony, or to
be a fugitive from justice.[31]

In civil matters, the sheriff may administer oaths to appraisers;[32]
and is authorized to make judicial sales (of which his proces verbal is

---

22. C. Cr. P., 1928, arts.
    567-571.
23. Rev. Stat., 1870, secs.
    1768, 3574.
24. Rev. Stat., 1870, secs.
    2841, 2842, 3577, 3578.
25. La. A., 1892, #85.
26. La. A., 1855, #121, sec. 8;
    Rev. Stat., 1870, sec. 2847.
    These laws refer to the state
    penitentiary then located in
    Baton Rouge. It has since
    been moved to Angola.
27. La. A., 1888, #121. This act
    does not, of course, refer to
    criminals sentenced to hard
    labor. A later act author-

ized the police jury to work
or hire out prisoners sentenced to imprisonment in the
parish prison. La. A., 1894,
#29; ibid., 1904, #191.
28. La. A., 1894, #156.
29. La. A., 1932, #80, sec. 2.
30. La. A., 1934, #197.
31. La. A., 1934, 1st E. S., #9,
    sec. 15. Such fingerprints
    are made in duplicate and
    both copies are sent to the
    state bureau of investiga-
    tion and identification.
32. La. A., 1855, #301, sec. 7;
    Rev. Stat., 1870, sec. 3543;
    C. P., 1870, art. 770.

an authentic act).[33] He also sells property for unpaid taxes and for-
wards such moneys to the state treasurer.[34] In an act providing for
tick eradication, the sheriff is authorized to sell at public auction,
after due advertisement, cattle found roaming at large.[35]

All funds of the registry of the court which may come into the
hands of the sheriff in any judicial proceedings and not belonging to
him are deposited in the bank designated by the police jury as the fiscal agent of the parish.[36] The sheriff is designated as trustee for
holders of rural mortgage bonds.[37]

Whenever elections are held in the parish, he provides suitable
ballot boxes for each polling place, and delivers to the commissioners
of election a list of registered voters who have secured their poll re-
ceipts.[38]

The records of the sheriff are kept in his office in the courthouse.

Civil

98.   CIVIL DOCKET, SHERIFF'S OFFICE, 1877-1909; July 31, 1928-Oct.
       15, 1928; May 1933--. 3 vols. (vol. 1928 labeled 1).
Record of services rendered by sheriff in civil, criminal, and probate
cases, 1877-1909, and civil suits 1928 and May 1933--. Civil suit records give the docket number, title of suit, date, type of papers, including citations, writs of seizure, advertising of sale, acts of sale,
commissions on sales, and serving of subpoenas. There is a notation
after each type of paper served mentioning whether served to the individual or left at his domicile. In some cases, charges to be collected
for the clerk of court and appraisers are also included. Criminal records give docket number, title of case, charge, cost of maintenance of

---

33. Or. Terr. A., 1805, XXV,
     secs. 9, 10; La. A., 1855,
     #337. In making such sales
     the sheriff must state in the
     deed of conveyance the amount
     of every special mortgage due
     thereon; cf. La. A., 1817, p.
     24, sec. 18.
34. In cases of seizure and sale
     to satisfy judgments for de-
     linquent taxes the sheriff
     was forbidden to seize other
     property than that designat-
     ed for the tax on the assess-
     ment roll; cf. La. A., 1877,
     E. S., #34, sec. 2. Sales
     of property for unpaid taxes
     are made at the courthouse
     door and should there be no

bid equal to the minimum,
the sheriff certifies this
fact to the state land office; cf. La. A., 1924,
#237; ibid., 1932, #64.
35. This law does not, however,
     apply in parishes having an
     open range ordinance. The
     net proceeds of such sales,
     if unclaimed within five
     days, are turned over to
     the state livestock sanitary
     board; cf. La. A., 1930, #6.
36. La. A., 1934, #39.
37. La. A., 1914, #176, sec. 3.
38. La. A., 1894, #181, sec. 20;
     ibid., 1922, #97, sec. 24;
     ibid., 1934, 1st E. S., #4,
     sec. 1.

prisoner, and charges for turnkey. Probate matters give docket number,
title of succession, and charges for advertising of sale, executing act
of sale, and commissions for auctioneer. The name of the attorney and
amount deposited to cover costs of services are mentioned in a few in-
stances. Chron. arr. and numer. by docket nos. No index. Hdw. Aver.
300 pp., 18 x 12 x 2.

    99. APPRAISEMENTS, SHERIFF'S OFFICE, 1875-1901. 1 vol. Discon-
          tinued.
Appraisals of property in litigation, giving date, title of suit, description of property, and amount of appraisement. Chron. arr. No index. Hdw. on printed forms. 160 pp., 18 x 12 x 2.

Criminal

    100. CRIMINAL COURT RECORD, June 25, 1929-Nov. 12, 1929. 1 vol.
          (1).
Record of subpoenas and other papers issued by the criminal district
court of Orleans Parish and served by the sheriff or deputies of St.
Bernard, giving the number and title of the case, date process received,
type of process, by whom served, date returned and to whom. Numer. arr.
by case no. and chron. by date process received under each case. No index. Hdw. 300 pp., 18 x 10 x 2.

    101. JAIL RECORD, 1877--. 2 vols. (1st vol. not labeled; 2nd vol.
          labeled 1). Title varies: Register of Prisoners.
Record of prisoners committed to jail, giving date of commitment, name,
color, sex, offense, date sentenced, term, where, i. e., state penitentiary or parish jail, date discharged and remarks. Chron. arr. No index. Hdw. Aver. 200 pp., 18 x 10 x 1.

    102. LEDGER, FINES AND DISBURSEMENTS, 1924-27. 1 vol.
Record of fines collected, giving date, case number, name of defendant,
amount of fine and to what fund credited. Also includes costs of court,
giving date, services charged for, including opening and closing of
court by sheriff, services of district attorney, and clerk of court,
giving the amount for service of each, debited to sheriff's salary fund.
Chron. arr. by date of entry. No index. Hdw. 284 pp., (only 13 pp.
are filled), 14 x 9 x 1.

    103. [SHERIFF'S MAINTENANCE ACCOUNT], 1918-22 in JOURNAL [Tax
          Funds], entry 111.
Record of maintenance of parish prisoners and incidental expenses of
the sheriff's office, giving date, item for which expenditure was made
and amount. Chron. arr. by date of entry. No index. Hdw.

Bibliographical Note

The great depository of primary source materials on the HRS is the National Archive's Record Group No. 69 ("Records of the Work Projects Administration"). A useful guide to this material is Betty Herscher, comp., *Preliminary Checklist of the Records of the Historical Records Survey, 1935–1942* (Washington, D.C.: National Archives, March, 1945). The Department of Archives, Louisiana State University, possesses several large boxes of material on the HRS in Louisiana; some of these documents (such as official correspondence and mimeographed progress reports) are found in duplicate in the National Archives, but more of them are items that evidently were never sent to (or received from) Washington, and they reveal much about the day-to-day operation of the state HRS. Appropriately for a staff that did its job well during the life of the Survey, Andreassen and his successors saw to it that their office files were placed in the state university's archives, where they have been sorted and filed and preserved in good condition, although they have scarcely been perused in the past twenty-five years.

The basic guide to all HRS publications is Sargent B. Child and Dorothy P. Holmes, *Bibliography of Research Project Reports: Check List of Historical Records Survey Publications*, WPA Technical Series, Research and Record Bibliography, No. 7, revised, (Washington, D.C.: Federal Works Agency, Works Projects Administration, Division of Service Projects, April, 1943). The Louisiana titles listed in this bibliography appear in John C. L. Andreassen, "Check List of Historical Records Survey and Survey of Federal Archives Publications for Louisiana," *Louisiana Historical Quarterly*, XXVII (April, 1944), 613–23.

Among the essays about the HRS published during the 1930s, several are notable as sheer description (and justification) of what the HRS was doing. Luther H. Evans, "The Historical Records Survey," in A. F. Kuhlman (ed.), *Public Documents* (Chicago: American Library Association, 1936), 209–214, is a reprint of Evans' statement on March 1, 1938, to a subcommittee of the Senate Committee on Education and Labor. Luther H. Evans, "The Local Archives Program of the WPA Historical Records Survey," in Jerome K. Wilcox and A. F. Kuhlman (eds.), *Public Documents with Archives and Libraries* (Chicago: American Library Association, 1938), 284–300, is an extension of Evans' remarks to the Senate committee made for a symposium on archives and libraries. A clear statement of just what Evans and his national editor thought a *record* was and what they felt the HRS ought do with it is Evans and Edythe Weiner, "The Analysis of County Records," *American Archivist*, I (October, 1938), 186–200.

In 1943, George W. Roach, the assistant supervisor of the New York State HRS from 1938 to 1942, published "Final Report: The Historical Records Survey in Upstate New York, 1936–1942," *New York History*, XXIV (January, 1943), 39–55. For the next thirty years, virtually nothing on the HRS in particular states appeared in print. Then in April, 1974, two state studies were published in a collection of essays on the HRS: Trudy Huskamp Peterson, "The Iowa Historical Records Survey, 1936–1942," and Chester W. Bowie, "The Wisconsin Historical Records Survey, Then and Now," both in *American Archivist*, XXXVII (April, 1974), 223–45, 247–61. This issue of *American Archivist* also contains two able essays by two archivists concerned with the neglect of the HRS by the past generation: Leonard Rapport, "Dumped from a Wharf into Casco Bay: The Historical Records Survey Revisited," 201–210; and Edward C. Papenfuse, " 'A Modicum of Commitment': The Present and Future Importance of the Historical Records Survey," 211–21. A year later, Iowa again gained attention— this time from the former state director of the Iowa HRS—in Don Farran, "The Historical Records Survey in Iowa, 1936–1942," *Annals of Iowa*, XLII (Spring, 1975), 597–608. Meantime, in 1958, David L. Smiley published a brief essay, "The W.P.A. Historical Records Survey," in William B. Hesseltine and Donald R. McNeil (eds.), *In Support of Clio: Essays in Memory of Herbert A. Kellar* (Madison: State Historical Society of Wisconsin, 1958), 3–28; he followed this with "A Slice of Life in Depression America: The Records of the Historical Records Survey," *Prologue*, III (Winter, 1971), 153–159.

The most comprehensive study of the HRS, by far, is that made by William F. McDonald in his huge administrative history of the WPA Arts Projects, *Federal Relief Administration and the Arts* (Columbus: Ohio State University Press, 1969). McDonald and a large staff of assistants actually wrote this tome during World War II, but it did not appear in print until 1969. Jerre Mangione, former national coordinating editor of the FWP, in his *The Dream and the Deal: The Federal Writers' Project, 1935–1943* (Boston: Little, Brown, 1972), notes that publication of McDonald's book was "held up for twenty years by a former official of the arts program who objected to some of its passages." Had it appeared earlier, McDonald's encyclopedic study might have provoked an earlier interest in the Four Arts program, which has of late finally begun to receive some attention from historians, who are now examining one by one each of the arts programs that McDonald's book surveyed from the perspective of the Washington administrators of these programs. The Writers' Project has received more attention than any of the other projects—as evidenced by Mangione's *The Dream and the Deal* and the numerous reviews and published commentary it evoked: Malcolm Cowley, "Federal Writers' Project," *New Republic*, October 21, 1972, pp. 22–26; Harold Rosenberg, "Anyone Who Could Write English," *New Yorker*, January 20, 1973, pp. 99–102; and Daniel Aaron, "A Giant Mirror for America," *Reviews in American History*, I (June, 1973), 277–281. The HRS has yet to receive a study comparable in scope and quality to that of Jane DeHart Mathews' book, *The Federal Theatre, 1935–1939: Plays, Relief, and Politics* (Princeton: Princeton University Press, 1967); or Richard D. McKinzie, *The New Deal for Artists* (Princeton: Princeton University Press, 1973); or Monty Noam Penkower, *The Federal Writers' Project: A Study in Government Patronage of the Arts* (Urbana: University of Illinois Press, 1977). I regard my own essay on the Louisiana HRS as a modest contribution to what may in time become a fuller body of historical literature on the Historical Records Survey.